ੴ ਸਤਿਗੁਰ ਪ੍ਰਸਾਦਿ।।

PEARLS
OF
SIKHISM

The whole realm of existence is created and governed by The Eternal Writ of God. His Will is All - Pervasive And Absolute. Under His Command the wind blows, the rivers flow and the sun and the moon move in their orbits. His supremacy is asserted over everything. By the Grace of such a Lord only, human souls are saved from the torments of transmigration.
We Salute His Might.

Sikh Missionary Center

Sikh Missionary Center
P.O. Box 62521
Phoenix, Arizona 85082 USA

Out of deep love and respect, to honor our Immaculate Lord, King of Kings, Guru Nanak we have tried to make an effort to describe His splendors. We apologize for any errors committed unconsciously which show disrespect to His Glory.

Sikh Missionary Center

Our Multiple Language Website:

www.sikhmissionary.net

ISBN: 978-0-9816672-0-1

Printed By: Sheridan Books, Inc.
Ann Arbor, Michigan, U.S.A.

CONTENTS

INTRODUCTION

Whenever you see a man with beard and turban, there are more than ninety percent chances that he is a Sikh from India.

In order to create public awareness about the Sikhs and Sikh Religion, this book is published and is being distributed among the general public.

Sikh Religion is the Fifth largest religion now in the world. There are about 22 to 25 million Sikhs living all over the world of which more than half million are living in the U.S.A.

May, 2008   Sikh Missionary Center

SIKH RELIGION

It is always believed that whenever the Righteousness vanishes from this world and the Falsehood takes its place, there has been a call from the Heaven to restore peace and justice on earth. Sayad Mohammad Latif (a Muslim writer) writes in his history of the Punjab (India), "Great jealousy and hatred existed in those days between the Hindus and the Mohammadans and the whole non-Muslim population was subject to persecution by the Mohammadan rulers." Bhai Gurdas, a Sikh scholar writes, "The Qazi (Muslim priest) who occupies the seat of justice, accepts bribe and then passes unjust orders." Guru Nanak describes the situation during the fifteen century as:

"Kings are butchers
Cruelty their knife, and
Sense of duty and responsibility have taken wings and vanished."
(Slok Mohalla 1, p-145 Guru Granth Sahib)

When the hour is the darkest, the coming of a Prophet is imminent. Out of the dark clouds of falsehood, hypocrisy, injustice, cruelty and bigotry, there came a ray of sunshine from the Heaven as described by Bhai Gurdas, a Sikh Apostle:

"Heaven at last heard the prayers of the people,
Guru Nanak was sent to the world.
The disciples met and drank the nectar of his Lotus feet,
And realized the Divine in this age of materialism.
Guru Nanak re-established Dharma,
All castes he merged into one race of man.
The rich and the poor he brought on one level,
From the Founder of Humanity a new race of love goes forth;
In humility they bow down to each other."
(Bhai Gurdas, Var 1- pauri 23)

Heaven at last heard the cries and prayers of the oppressed and there appeared the Savior of Humanity, Prophet of Peace, Fountain of Heavenly Love and Ocean of Virtue in the name of Guru Nanak, the founder of Sikh Religion.

SIKH RELIGION

Sikh Religion was founded by Guru Nanak in the form of ten Gurus (1469-1708) in India. The tenth Master, Guru Gobind Singh ended the personal Guruship and proclaimed Guru Granth Sahib (Sikh Holy Scripture) as the last Guru for ever.

Guru Granth Sahib was written and compiled by the Gurus themselves and hence it is authentic. Nobody is allowed to change even a comma or a period in it (1430 pages).

Guru Granth Sahib does not narrate the life story of the Gurus but it is wholly dedicated to the Glory of the Almighty God only. **Sikhism is not a blend or reproduction of earlier religions but it is a New Revelation altogether.** The teachings that the Gurus gave to this world, came DIRECT to them from God which the Gurus Confirm:

"This Word comes from Him Who hath created the world."
(Slok Mohalla 4, p-306 Guru Granth Sahib)

To attain salvation, Sikhism rejects all fasts, rites and rituals. It rejects the claims of Yoga, mortification of body, self-torture, penances and renunciation. Sikhism does not believe in the worship of gods and goddesses, stones, statues, idols, pictures, tombs or crematoriums. Only One God, The Formless, is to be Glorified.

The Gurus preached Sikh Religion strictly as monotheistic requiring belief in none other than One Supreme Being only.

GURU - THE DIVINE LIGHT:

The word 'Guru' is so popular in India that in order to understand the fundamental concept of 'guru' in Sikhism, one must first completely drive out of one's mind the prevalent popular notion of a guru. The popular term 'guru' often used for a Brahmin, a yogic teacher or a guide or even a school teacher, has made the Guruship so cheap that a scholar describes these gurus as 'wicks which smell foul after the lamps are extinguished.'

The term 'Guru' in Sikhism is not used for a teacher or guide or an expert or even a human body. The word 'Guru' is composed of two terms:

GU - means darkness, and

RU - means light

In Sikhism the word 'Guru' is, therefore, defined as the Light that dispels all darkness, and that is called JOT (Divine Light).

God was sitting alone in an Absolute trance before the world was created and Sikhism refers to Him as the Guru:

"How shall I utter the Glory of the Guru,

For, the Guru is Ever-awake Spring of Truth

In prime and beginning of the ages and all the ages through

He is the Perfect Lord God."

(Asa Mohalla 5, p- 397, Guru Granth Sahib)

(All quotations are from Guru Granth Sahib (GGS) unless it is noted otherwise.)

The Guru is the Divine Light of the three worlds:

"The Guru is the Beneficent, the Sanctuary of Peace,

The Light of the three worlds."

(Slok Moh. 1, p-137)

What are the three worlds? One world is what is above us to infinity, the second world is what is below us to infinity and the third world is what is at our level to infinity. The Divine Light (Guru) which is all-pervading and shines over all the three worlds, caused Himself to be called, 'Guru Nanak':

"Guru, the Embodiment of Divine Light has caused
Himself to be called Guru Nanak":
(Swayai Moh. 5, p-1408)

Guru Nanak was, therefore, the Embodiment of Divine Light. HE WAS BORN GURU:
"Guru Nanak is embodiment of the Light of God."
(Basant Moh. 5, p-1192)

Thus Guru in Sikhism is a perfect Prophet or Messenger of God in whom the Light of God shines fully, visibly and completely. Guru is in union with the Divine. Thus he ushers the devotees, the seekers of Truth into a spiritual birth. Through him the Glory of the Lord is transmitted to humanity. On account of his Divine prerogatives, the Guru, though human in form, is Divine in spirit.

When Guru Nanak conferred Guruship on Bhai Lehna (his devotee later called Guru Angad Dev), the Jot was passed on and Guru Angad Dev too became the embodiment of Divine Light. After conferring Guruship, Guru Nanak himself bowed before Guru Angad Dev. He did not bow to the body of Guru Angad Dev but he bowed before the Divine Light (Guru) which he passed on by his Divine Power. In the same way all the nine Gurus were the embodiments of Gur Nanak Jot (Divine Light). The tenth Master, Guru Gobind Singh ended personal Guruship and then conferred Guruship on the Adi Granth (Sikh Holy Scripture), which too became the embodiment of Divine Light and was called Guru Granth Sahib. **Guru Gobind Singh then bowed before Guru Granth Sahib and asked his Sikhs to do so. He did not bow before a book (or Granth) but he bowed before the Divine Light (Guru) which he passed on to the Adi Granth by his Divine Power. Gur Nanak Jot is, therefore,**

enshrined and preserved in Guru Granth Sahib, and it is the Living
Guru for ever (present as well as future). For the Sikhs, the Guru
Granth is the manifestation of the Guru's Spirit and through it ,
Guru Nanak lives on in the Sikh Faith.

Guru Nanak never said to anyone that he could go to heaven
or get salvation only if he had become his disciple. Being embodiment of Divine Light, and as the Divine Light knows no boundaries
and does not belong to any particular sect or religion, so he stood
guarantee to the entire humanity that whosoever one may be irrespective of caste, creed, race, sex, color, religion or nationality,
'Whosoever meditates upon One God, the Formless, will get salvation':
"He shall become pure whosoever repeateth His Name
With devotion, affection and heartfelt love."
(Gauri Sukhmani Moh. 5, p-290)

GURU NANAK DEV (1469-1539 A.D)

Guru Nanak was born in 1469 at Rai Bhoeki Talwandi now known
as Nankana Sahib situated in Punjab province of Pakistan. This place is
about 55 miles north-west of Lahore. His father, Mehta Kalu was a Patwari-
an accountant of land revenue in the government. Guru's mother was Mata
Tripta and he had one older sister, Bibi Nanki. From the very childhood,
Bibi Nanki saw in him the Light of God but she did not reveal this secret to
anyone. She is known as the first disciple of Guru Nanak.

GURU'S SCHOOLING:

At the age of seven, Guru Nanak was sent to school, which was run by a teacher, Pandit Gopal Das, at his village. As usual the teacher started the lesson with an alphabet but the teacher was wonder-struck when the Guru asked him to explain the meanings of the letters of the alphabet. However at the helplessness of his teacher, the Guru wrote the meanings of each and every letter of the alphabet. **This was the first Divine Message delivered by Guru Nanak. This was an explanation of deeper truth about human beings and God and the way to realize God in terms of the alphabet.** The teacher stood abashed before the Divine Master and bowed to him. He then took him back to his father and said, "Mehtaji, your son is an Avtar (prophet) and has come to redeem the victims of Kalyug (the age of Falsehood). He is destined to be a world Teacher, there is nothing that I can teach him."

(The above Divine Message is included in Guru Granth Sahib at page 432 as Raag Asa Mohalla 1, Pati Likhi).

COBRA SERVES THE DIVINE MASTER:

As usually is the case in villages, the father sent his son to graze the buffaloes in the pastures who fell asleep under the shade of a tree. As the sun rose higher, the shadow moved away. A big cobra came out of its den and provided shadow with its hood over the face of the Divine Master. Rai Bular, an officer-in-charge of the area, happened to pass by that side with his attendants. When he saw this strange scene, he was convinced that the boy was a man of God. Upon seeing the people, the Cobra retreated to its den and Rai Bular touched Guru's feet in great reverence and thus became Guru's disciple.

GURU'S MARRIAGE:

In order to bring him around the worldly affairs, the next step came the marriage. The marriage date is given different in different Janamsakhis (biographies), and it is presumed that he was between 14 to 18 years of age when he got married. His wife, Sulakhni, was the daughter of Bhai Mula, a resident of Batala in Gurdaspur district. She gave birth to two sons, Sri Chand and Lakhmi Das.

His father soon found out that even the married life did not divest him of his pre-occupation with matters pertaining to his Divine mission. As a matter of fact, his concept of duty was not to serve himself and his family rather to transcend it so that the self might participate in the divine scheme of things and spiritualize the whole world around him. Humanity was his family and serving the humanity was the service of the Lord. Bhai Gurdas writes that the Guru saw the whole world in flames; flames of falsehood, tyranny, hypocrisy and bigotry. He had to go and extinguish that fire with eternal love, truth and dedication. He had the divine mission to teach to humanity, the lesson of the brotherhood of mankind and the fatherhood of God. "The Primal Being created the Light; all men are the creation of Providence: all human beings have sprung from one Light. Who, then, is bad and who is good?" (Parbhati-Kabir, p-1349-50)

TRAVELS OF GURU NANAK:

Guru Nanak Dev saw the world suffering out of hatred, fanaticism, falsehood and hypocrisy. The world had sunk in wickedness and sin. So he set out for the regeneration of humanity on this earth. He carried the torch of truth, heavenly love, peace and joy for mankind. He embarked on his Divine Mission and went towards east, west, north and south and visited various centers of Hindus, Muslims, Buddhists, Jainis, Sufis, Yogis and Sidhas. He met people of different religions, tribes, cultures and races. He traveled on foot for 14 years with his Muslim companion named Mardana, a minstrel. His travels are called Udasis.

In his first Udasi (travel), Guru Nanak covered east and south of India and returned home after spending a little more than eight years. He started from Sultanpur in August, 1507 and went to his village Talwandi to meet and inform his parents about his long journey. The old parents wanted comfort and protection from their young son in their old age and so they asked him not to go. But there were thousands and thousands others waiting for the Divine Master for comfort, love and salvation. The Guru, therefore, told his parents, "There is a call from Heaven, I must go whither He directs me to go."

FIRST STOP AT EMINABAD:

Accompanied by Mardana, the Guru embarked on his mission and left his family behind. He made his first stop at Saidpur, now known as Eminabad, and there he met a poor carpenter named Lalo. The Master looked at poor Lalo graciously and he was blessed with Divine love and lo, he was a blessed man. The Guru chose to stay with Lalo for sometimes as a guest. The news reached Malik Bhago, the chief of the town, that a holy person was staying with Lalo. Malik Bhago was a corrupt man and he had amassed wealth through unfair means. He held a big gathering and invited all holy men including the Guru. The Guru, however, did not accept his invitation. Malik then made a special arrangement for the Guru and requested him to come and eat at his residence. At last the Guru went there and Malik Bhago said, "O holy man, I have prepared so many dishes for you, but you are staying with a poor carpenter and eating his dry bread. Please stay with me." The Guru replied, "I cannot eat your food because your bread is earned by dishonest means while Lalo's bread is made from the hard-earned money." This made Malik Bhago very mad and he asked the Guru to prove his point. The Guru then sent for a loaf of bread from Lalo's house. In one hand the Guru held Lalo's bread and in the other that of Malik Bhago's, and when he squeezed both, milk came out from Lalo's bread and blood dripped from Malik Bhago's bread. Malik Bhago was completely shaken by his guilt and asked for forgiveness. The Guru asked him to distribute his ill-gotten wealth among the poor and henceforth live a honest life. Malik Bhago was re-born with the Guru's blessing.

He then went towards the east and reached Assam Province beyond Calcutta. He visited various famous Hindu Pilgrimage places and Temples like Hardwar, Gorakhmata, Banaras, Gaya and Kamrup. **The**

Guru preached against superstitions and rituals, worship of gods and goddesses, penances and renunciation. He stressed that only One God, the Formless, was to be glorified. In this way he showed the path of truth and enlightenment.

GURU TO SANGLADEEP (CEYLON - SRI LANKA):

Guru went towards south and after visiting the famous Temple of Jagan Nath Puri, he reached Matiakalam (now known as Matalai) which was the capital of Sangladeep under Raja Shiv Nabh.

Bhai Mansukh, a trader from Punjab and a disciple of the Guru, had been to Sangladeep in connection with his business long before the Guru's visit to the island. By reason of his trade, Bhai Mansukh had access to Raja Shiv Nabh and thus he had told the Raja all about Guru Nanak. The Raja asked how he could meet the Guru. Mansukh told him, "Rise early in the morning and recite Moolmantar. (see in Appendix under Glossary). If you earnestly pray, the Guru will respond to your prayers."

Every morning Raja Shiv Nabh meditated and prayed for the holy sight (darshan) of the Guru. Time passed on but the Guru did not appear. Many persons came and claimed to be the Guru but all were found to be the fake claimants. One day news was brought to the Raja that a holy man, with a rare glory beaming on his face (spiritual aura), had arrived in the old neglected garden, and as soon as he set his foot in the garden, the withered trees sprouted into green foliage.

Due to the previous fake claimants, the Raja devised a plan to test the visitors before he could bow his head to any one of them. The Raja, therefore, sent beautiful girls to seduce the new-comer with their beauty and charm. The report was sent to the Raja that the girls not only failed to seduce the visitor, but they themselves had been transformed under his spell. Hearing this, the Raja hurriedly came to see the holy Master. Spontaneously he fell at the feet of the Guru. The Guru placed his hand on his head and blessed him. Who could describe the ecstatic joy that had dawned upon Raja.

The whole city rushed to the garden to have holy sight of the Master. A dharamsala, a religious common place, was built where the Guru held daily religious congregations and preached his divine doctrine. People were enlightened with God's Name and they became Guru's followers.

GURU TO KAILASH PARBAT:

After coming from the South, the Guru went towards North and entered into Tibet and then proceeded to the Mansarovar Lake and Kailash Parbat (also called Sumeir Parbat). There he met many renowned Sidhas. They asked the Guru about the conditions prevailing in India. The Guru informed them that falsehood overshadowed the land and the moon of truth was completely enshrouded in the darkness of ignorance. The kings were butchers and justice had taken wings and flown away. Then he further said,"Nathji, when the Sidhas (Yogis) are hiding themselves in mountain enclaves, who is left over there to lead the people in the right direction?"

The Sidhas wanted the young Guru to wear their garb and become a yogi, but they could not succeed. They had the supernatural powers which they tried upon the Guru. They asked him to bring water from the nearby spring. The Guru took a bowl and went to bring water. By their miraculous powers, the Sidhas turned the water into jewels and diamonds. They had thought that the Guru would be overwhelmed with the wealth. But he did not care about the jewels and came back with empty bowl. They still tried many more tricks but failed to succeed. At last they acknowledged the super-powers of the Guru and sat around him in submission and the discussion ensued. The Guru convinced them that instead of wearing empty forms and doing hard penances, they should exert themselves in the service of mankind.

(The discussion with Sidhas is given in Guru Granth Sahib as 'Sidh Gost' starting on page 938).

The Guru then proceeded to Multan, Uch, Sakhar and reached Lakhpat, where a Gurdwara stands marking the memory of the Guru. Then he reached Kuriani where a tank is called after Guru's name. He visited Miani, about fifty miles west of city of Karachi and visited the temples of Hindus and the Muslims in the area. Near Hinglaj, there is a Dharmsala preserving the memory of the Guru's visit to this place. From there he boarded a ship for Arabia.

GURU NANAK AT MECCA:

He disguised himself in the blue dress of a Mohammadan pilgrim, took a faqir's staff in his hand and a collection of his hymns called 'Pothi' under his arm. He also carried with him like a Muslim devotee, a cup for his ablutions and a rug whereon to pray. Like a pilgrim he went inside the great mosque where the pilgrims were engaged in their devotions. When he lay down to sleep at night, he turned his feet towards the Kaaba. Jiwan, a priest, kicked him and said, "Who is this infidel sleeping with his feet towards the House of God?" The Guru replied, "Turn my feet in the direction in which God is not." Upon this Jiwan seized the Guru's feet and dragged them in the opposite direction. Whereupon, it is said, the Kaaba (temple) turned around, and followed the revolution of Guru's body. Those who witnessed this miracle were astonished and saluted the Guru as a supernatural being. (Jiwan came in the morning to sweep the floor of the mosque).

Then the Qazis and the Mullas crowded around the Guru and asked whether he was a Muslim or a Hindu? The Guru replied that he was neither of the two. Then they asked, "Who is the superior of the two, the Hindu or the Muslim?" The Guru replied, "Without good deeds, both will repent. The superiority lies in deeds and not in mere creeds."

The chief priest was a seeker of the Truth and he asked for Guru's blessings. The Guru preached the doctrine of Nam. He then gave instructions to the priest in the art of true living, to practice to live in His presence day and night and to glorify the Lord and thereby to rub out the dirt of sins from the tablet of the mind.

GURU AT MEDINA:

In due time the Guru proceeded to Medina, another holy city of the Muslims where their Prophet Mohammad lived for many years and breathed his last. He reached at nightfall and stopped outside the town. It happened to be a place where lepers were segregated and no provision was made for their comfort or treatment. History states that the Guru healed them all and as a result, the people came in crowds to have holy glimpse of the Guru. After that he journeyed to Baghdad through Basra. (visit to Baghdad is described in later chapters).

LIVING BY HONEST MEANS:

Emphasis were laid on honest hard labor for living. Asceticism was explicitly rejected and instead a disciplined worldliness and family life was set forth as the proper course. Earnest living through honest hard labor and then out of that hard earned money, giving in the name of the Lord, was the moral way to bring up the family.

The Guru himself set up this example by working with his hands in the fields for the remaining about 18 to 20 years of his life at Kartarpur. He emphasized this course in the following Sabad:

"Men without divine knowledge sing hymns.
The Hungry Mulla maketh a home of his mosque.
One who earneth nothing slitteth his ears;
Another becometh a beggar and loseth his caste.
Touch not at all the feet of those
Who call themselves gurus and pirs, and go begging.
They who eat the fruit of their labor and bestow something

in the name of Lord,
O Nanak, recognize the right way."
(Sarang ki Var, Slok Mohalla 1, p-1245)

BHAI LEHNA:

As the time of Guru's departure (from the world) was drawing near, it was becoming clear to Mataji (Guru's wife) that there would be succession to Guruship. As is the custom in the world, she always thought that her sons should be the heir of their father's property, the Guruship. One day she said to the Guru, "My Lord, keep my sons in mind." This meant that the Guruship should be passed on to one of her sons. The Guru said, "Bring your sons." Both the sons were brought before the Guru. He then threw a bowl in a tank of muddy water, and asked his eldest son, Sri Chand, to go and recover the bowl from the tank. Sri Chand replied, "Why did you throw the bowl, if it had to be brought back?" So he refused to do the job. In the same way the younger son declined to act. Then the Guru turned to his devotee Bhai Lehna and said,"Lehnaji, go and bring the bowl." Bhai Lehna said,"Sat bachan (Yes Sir)." Bhai Lehna went and recovered the bowl without caring for his clothes getting soiled with mud. There were a few more tests like this between his sons and Bhai Lehna.

The moral as the Guru enunciated here is that a Sikh must make a total unconditional surrender before the Guru. He must have total obedience for the Guru's order, then and only then the Sikh reaches his goal i.e becomes one with Him. The Guru's sons questioned him at every step, while Bhai Lehna submitted willfully without uttering even one word. The result being that Bhai Lehna was blessed with Guruship and became the embodiment of Divine Light.

According to Guru's mandate and code of conduct, a Sikh must lead spiritual and moral life while conducting every day's business to earn Guru's blessing. The Guru's mandate is clear:
"By obeying His order, man is acceptable

And shall then reach the Lord's court."
(Asa di Var- pauri 15, p-471)

ASCENSION OF GURU NANAK:

On September 2, 1539 (2 Asu, 1596 Asu vadi 5) Guru Nanak placed five Paise (Indian currency) before Bhai Lehna and bowed to him in token of his succession to the Guruship. He placed the umbrella of Spiritual Sovereignty over Bhai Lehna's head. **Thus, he created another Guru Nanak and called him GURU ANGAD DEV.**

"Jot uha jugat sai seih kaya feir paltiai."
(Ramkali ki Var- Rai Balwand, p-966)
'Divine Light is the same
The Way and Mode are the same
The Master has merely changed the body.'
(Translation of the above)
When Guruship was passed on to Guru Angad, people realized that Guru Nanak was soon to depart bodily from the world (As a Divine Light and Spirit, the Guru is always present). The Sikhs, the Hindus and the Muslims came from all over to have holy glimpse of Guru Nanak.

Guru's Muslim devotees wanted to bury him after his death. His Hindu followers desired to cremate his body. When the Guru was asked for his decision, he replied, "Let the Hindus place flowers on my right and the Muslims on my left. Those whose flowers are found fresh in the morning, may have the disposal rights of my body."

The Guru drew a sheet over him. When the sheet was removed next morning, body was not found underneath, but the flowers on both sides were afresh. **The light blended with Light and the spirit went back and merged with the Master Spirit**. It confirms that the Guru was not a body but it was the Divine Light.

The Hindus and the Muslims removed their respective flowers and cut the sheet into two. The former cremated the sheet and the latter buried it. It happened at Kartarpur on September 22, 1539 (23rd day of Asu, Vadi 10, Sambat 1596). He was about seventy and a half years of age.

The Sikhs built a Gurdwara and the Muslims a tomb in his honor on the bank of river Ravi. Both had since been washed away by the river, perhaps by a super act, so as to avoid idolatrous worship of the Guru's last resting place.

Rituals and superstitions earned the sanctions of old times. Religion had degenerated into ceremonial acts only. The life and teachings of Guru Nanak offer consistent evidence of fruitlessness of rituals. He exposed their hollowness and exhorted human beings to rise above such customs. Guru Nanak's religion excluded all senseless dogmas and meaningless rituals. **With no sword nor stick but armed with Divine Word, he preached that only Impersonal Absolute is to be worshiped. Any religion which does not guard its values, indicates a lower level of development and is deemed to disappear in the long run.**

GURU ANGAD DEV
(1504-1552, Guruship, 1539-1552)

GURU AMAR DAS
(1479-1574, Guruship, 1552-1574)

GURU RAM DAS
(1534-1581, Guruship, 1574-1581)

GURU ARJAN DEV
(1563-1606, Guruship 1581-1606)

Guru Arjan was born in Goindwal, a small town in Amritsar district, on April 15, 1563. He was the youngest son of Guru Ram Das and Bibi Bhani. As a child, one day he found his way to the bed of Guru Amar Das who was then resting. His mother ran to fetch the child before he could disturb the Guru, but he had already awakened the Guru, who revealed, "Let him come to me; 'yeh mera dohita bani ka bohita howega'- this grandson of mine shall be a ship to take mankind across the ocean of the world."

COMPLETION OF CONSTRUCTION WORK:

Mian Mir, a famous Muslim saint, was a friend and a devotee of the Guru. The Guru asked Mian Mir to lay the foundation stone of Hari Mandar which is now called Golden Temple, Amritsar (India).

When the construction of the tank and the temple was completed, Guru Arjan uttered the following Sabad in joy and gratitude to the Almighty:
"The Creator stood in the midst of the work,
And not a hair of any man's head was touched.
The Guru maketh my ablution successful......................."
(Sorath Mohalla 5, p-623)

COMPILATION OF THE ADI GRANTH:

Guru Arjan felt the need to lay down rules to guide his followers in their daily religious duties. He made plans for the compilation of Adi Granth. For that purpose he chose a secluded spot outside the city of Amritsar which is now called Ramsar. He got a tank excavated there. Tents were erected for the accommodation. Guru Arjan took abode near the tank and dictated hymns to Bhai Gurdas who wrote them down. The verses were arranged according to Raags or musical measures. The hymns of the first Guru came first then those of the second Guru and so on. After the Bani of the Gurus, came the verses of the Bhagats or the Indian saints. **(see below about Bhagats under Bhakti Movement and also about Bhats).**

A Muslim might never like to read a hymn of a Hindu saint, and by the same token a Hindu might not like to hear the religious verse of a Muslim saint. The Hindus did not allow a Hindu saint born in low caste family, to enter the Hindu temple. Such was the religious fanaticism prevailing at that time. **Guru Arjan, therefore, created an ocean in which all rivers and rivulets could fall and assume the appearance of the ocean itself. The composition of such an ocean was completed on Bhadon Vadi 1, Sambat 1661 (August 15, 1604 A.D.) and was called the Adi Granth. It was by no means a bible for the Sikhs alone, but it is universal in character. It contained no life story of the Gurus but only the Eternal Truth, each and every word of which was dedicated to the Glory of the Almighty God only.**

On Bhadon Sudi first, Sambat 1661 (August 30, 1604), Adi Granth was installed in the Hari Mandar (Golden Temple, Amritsar) and Bhai Buddha was appointed as the first Granthi (priest). Guru Granth Sahib is opened at random and first passage is read from top of left-hand side page and it is considered as the Divine Order of the day. The following Order came on that day:

"God Himself has come to Fulfill the Task of His Saints;
He Himself has Come to Do our Tasks.
And, now Blessed is the Pool of the earth and the (God's) Nectar
with which it is filled............................."

(Suhi Moh. 5, p-783)

Bhakti Movement:

Guru Arjan Dev compiled Sikh Scripture which included besides

Golden Temple, Amritsar

the compositions of the Gurus, the hymns of 15 Hindu and Muslim saints with their 778 verses. (The fifteen Bhagats in chronological order were Bhagat Sheikh Farid, Jai Dev, Trilochan, Nam Dev, Sadhna, Ramanand, Ravi Das, Sain, Kabir, Dhana, Pipa, Surdas, Bhikhan, Parmanand and Bhagat Beni). While including those hymns he applied certain norms. He incorporated only those hymns of these saints which were in agreement and in accordance with those of the Gurus in their meaning and Divine status. These Bhagats or saints believed in God because they felt oneness with Him emotionally and had faith and conviction in His existence rather than seeking any rational or intellectual explanation. They had deep devotion and immense love for the Divine. All the Bhagats were enlightened people. They spread the Divine message in different parts of India during twelfth to sixteenth centuries. Their hymns were soaked in pious morality with spiritual color and were filled with glorious praises of the Lord's Name. The devotional hymns of these saints along with their dedication and loyalty to the Lord, gave rise to Bhakti movement. This movement became means of providing spiritual and intellectual strength to people in medieval India. Bhakti movement was at its peak during fourteenth and fifteenth centuries. Devotees of God who belonged by birth to poor and low class families, were in spiritual height. Because of their intoxication for the Divine ideal, the hymns of these saints from the lower and poor status of the society earned space in Sikh Scripture. Bhakti is the yearning of the soul for union with the Divine in which separation from the Eternal amounts to torment of the inner-self. It is the emotional absorption into God which comes through ceaseless remembrance of the Name and rejoicing in His Glory. **Their hymns were so saturated with love of God that by including them in Sikh Scripture, Guru Arjan Dev gave them a status of Bani (Word) thus providing them a place of respect in Sikh Faith. By doing so Sikhism crossed the barriers of region and religion.** Those were disturbed times. Pages of history suggest that some of these saints not only themselves suffered cruelties and humiliation from the Muslim invaders and kings of those times but encouraged common people to bravely face pain and suffering to gain justice. Their compositions played great role in saving masses of people from moral and physical breakdown under the rule of Muslim tyrants. They guided the lives of the people of their times into fruitful spiritual channels and gave them moral anchor and support. They tried to undo oppressive and exploitative actions of the Muslim rulers. Such an endeavor on the part of these saints was the need of the time when India was in an era of political upheaval and social turmoil. The social structure based on the caste system was neither challenged before nor was the exploitation of the lower castes by the higher ones condemned. Bhagat Kabir and Bhagat Namdev severely criticized Brahmins for their insistence on ritualism and for their intolerance of any one who dared to find fault with their methods. Bhagat Kabir had been the most revolutionary of all the saints of Bhakti movement.

Bhats or Minstrels:

Bhats were a group of eleven Brahmins by caste and were closely related to each other. They were Bhat Kal Sahar, Gayand, Bhikha, Kirat, Mathura, Jalap, Salh, Bhalh, Balh, Harbans and Bhat Nath. History traces back their origin to Kaushik Rishi. They were mentally enlightened, intelligent and literary people. Since they were intellectual men, they composed their own ballads and would sing them to amuse themselves. From their writings it is evident that they wandered from place to place in search of a spiritual preceptor who could guide them towards the divine path. They were virtuous and righteous class of men and had an appetite for the divine. Cutting across the boundaries of mind and intellect these Bhats wanted to achieve celestial happiness. Intellectual pursuit did not interest them. Rather they wanted to have inner peace and comfort for their souls. During their journey while looking for a holy guide, they met a lot of hypocrites in the garb of saints. But found that their prayers, fasts and pilgrimages were designed to earn them money and not to save their souls. Those were just mechanical acts serving no spiritual purpose. They observed hypocrisy in the priesthood. On their way the Bhats met some true and sincere religious people also. But due to imperfections inherent in human beings these religious individuals could not attain the same mental stage as that of a true Guru, thereby giving dissatisfaction to the Bhats. These religious people were neither pure nor faultless. None could lead their souls to the Timeless Absolute One.

It was during their search that these Bhats reached Goindwal (Place in Punjab province in India) where Guru Arjan Dev was seated on the Divine Throne of Guru Nanak. They met Guru Arjan Dev around 1581 A.D. Meeting the Guru, their spiritual thirst was quenched. They found peace of mind in Guru Arjan's court. In the holy company of the Guru, they reached a step upwards on spiritual ladder which prompted them to write the glory of the Divine. The writings of the eleven Bhats matched with the ideal of Adi Granth and thus Guru Arjan Dev included them in the Sikh Scripture. Their compositions are called Swaiyas, a poetic form in which with deep respect and devotion they lauded the Gurus as the embodiment of Divine Light in very rich terms. They have written 121 Swaiyas in praise of the first five Gurus which are incorporated in Guru Granth Sahib along with other Bhagats' verses. Meeting with Guru Arjan, Bhat Bhika expressed his mental stage in one of his Swaiyas. He states that he wandered for full one year before he met Guru Arjan but could not find the righteous path. Bhats called the Gurus- Divine incarnations, holy preceptors and the physical manifestations of the Lord. In their verses the Bhats have mentioned that the spiritual light of Guru Nanak continued to be transferred to the other Gurus as one candle were to lit from another. All Gurus though different in body, were one in spirit. They saw image of God in the Gurus and felt blessed. Their minds and souls settled in peace and all their pains were annulled. Through Swaiyas they thanked the Lord for enabling them to reach that state of mind. They sang admirations of the divine light pervading in the Gurus and thus attained perfect bliss. In their Swaiyas they wrote whatever they saw and experienced in Guru Arjan Dev. They showed their enthusiasm and devotion in beautiful language and sang their own compositions with soul touching sentiments. With emotions saturated with love and adorations they praised the Gurus in terms of

Divine Light.

Some of the lines of their Swaiyas are recited in Harimandar Sahib at Amritsar by the devotees as Guru Granth Sahib is installed in the early hours of every morning. Thus the entire congregation pays tribute to the Guru in a unique manner. Some scholars believe that in the same way Bhats used to sing those laudatory compositions before Guru Arjan as the Adi Granth was placed in Harimandar Sahib each morning. After the Bhats had gone, their descendants used to sing those verses. Now the Sikhs pay their tribute to the Guru by singing those hymns. It is recorded in history that these Bhats had their own Bahis (registers) in which they had listed their daily events and writings. **All the contributors of Guru Granth Sahib have immortalized themselves through their compositions as their hymns were blessed with the status of Bani (Word) by Guru Arjan Dev..**

MARTYRDOM OF GURU ARJAN:

During the spiritual reign of Guru Arjan, crowds embraced Sikhism in Punjab and in various other parts of India and even in the neighboring countries. Many hilly Rajas became Guru's Sikhs. Guru's fame and influence was widely spread.

The following events lead to Guru's martyrdom:

The fourth Guru gave Guruship to his youngest son and upon this the eldest son (Prithi Chand) became very angry. Prithi Chand opposed his brother (Guru Arjan) throughout his life and tried to harm him at every step.

Chandu lal was a financial advisor to the Emperor of India. He had a daughter who was of marriageable age. He sent his family priest and barber to find a match for the girl. They searched and searched and ultimately found Guru Arjan's son (Har Gobind) as an excellent match for the girl. They reported and gave Chandu their analysis on the excellence of

Har Gobind and the enormous respect that his father (Guru) was commanding in the city of Amritsar. Chandu was not pleased hearing the praises of the Guru, so he used some derogatory remarks distinguishing himself and the Guru. Somehow the news of Chandu's ill remarks reached the Sikhs. The whole Sikh congregation decided and requested the Guru not to accept the alliance of haughty head like Chandu. The Guru had to accept the decision of the Sikh congregation and respectfully denied the relation of Chandu. He got very angry and became an ally of Prithi Chand to harm the Guru.

The Mughal Emperor Akbar had nominated his grandson Khusro in supersession of his son Jahangir. However Jahangir became the Emperor after Akbar's death. Khusro claimed the provinces of Punjab and Afghanistan. Jahangir unwilling to concede to this demand, ordered Khusro's arrest. Khusro escaped and fled towards Afghanistan. On the way he visited the Guru and begged the Guru for financial assistance. In Guru's house a friend or foe is treated equally. Prithi Chand & company concocted a story of Khusro being favored by the Guru to rouse the ire of Emperor Jahangir which added fuel to the blazing fire.

Guru's increasing influence to convert crowds of Hindus and Muslims to Sikhism, created a stir in the minds of the Pundits (Hindu Brahmins) and Qazis (Muslim priests). The compilation of the Adi Granth was considered a serious blow to other religions. Through all these circumstances Guru Arjan fell a victim to the bigotry and inhumanity of the Mughal Emperor.

Finally Jahangir ordered the Guru to pay two lakhs of rupees (two hundred thousand rupees) as fine, and also to erase the hymns in his Granth which were opposed to the Hindu and Muslim religions.

The Guru replied, "Whatever money I have is for the poor, the friendless and the stranger. If you ask for money, you may take whatever I have; but if you ask for it by way of fine I shall not give you even a penny, because a fine is imposed on the wicked worldly persons and not on priests and saints. As regarding the erasure of hymns in the Adi Granth, I cannot erase or alter an iota. I am a worshipper of the Immortal God.

There is no monarch save Him; and what He revealed to the Gurus, from Guru Nanak to Guru Ram Das, and afterwards to myself, is written in the holy Granth. The hymns contained in the Adi Granth are not disrespectful to any Hindu incarnation or any Mohammadan prophet. It is certainly stated that prophets, priests, and incarnations are the handiwork of the Immortal God, Whose limit none can find. My main object is to spread the truth and the destruction of falsehood; and if, in pursuance to this objective, this perishable body is to depart, I shall account it great good fortune."

When the Sikhs of Lahore came to know about the fine of two lakhs of rupees, they decided to raise the money to discharge the Guru's obligation of fine. The Guru issued a stern warning to his Sikhs that whosoever contributed to pay the fine imposed on him, would not be his Sikh. It was a matter of principle as mentioned in the Guru's reply above, and not a matter of two lakhs of rupees. The Qazis and Brahmins offered alternatives to the Guru to exchange death for expunging the alleged objectionable passages in Adi Granth and inserting the praises of Mohammad and of the Hindu deities. The Guru did not budge from his position.

Chandu was incharge and he made Guru Arjan sit on the red hot iron pan and burning sand was poured over his bare body. Guru's body was burning and was full of blisters.

His friend and devotee, Mian Mir, a Muslim saint, rushed to see him. When Mian Mir saw the ghastly scene, he cried out and said,"O Master! I cannot bear to see these horrors inflicted on thee. If you permit me, I would demolish this tyrant rule (Mian Mir is said to have felt supernatural powers at that time)."

The Guru smiled and asked Mian Mir to look towards the skies. It is said that Mian Mir saw Angels begging the Guru's permission to destroy the wicked and the proud.

The Guru addressed Mian Mir, "Mian Mir, you are perturbed too soon. **This is the Will of my Master (God), and I cheerfully submit and surrender to His Sweet Will." The Guru repeated and exemplified in action the meaning of this verse:**

"Tera kia meetha lagei
Har Nam padarath Nanak mangei."
(Asa Mohalla 5, p-394)
'Sweet be Thy Will, my Lord
Nanak beseecheth the gift of Nam.'
(Translation of the above)
The Guru bore all this torture with equanimity and never uttered a sigh or a groan.
The Guru was unruffled!
The Guru remained calm and unperturbed like a sea!
The Guru was in Absolute Bliss!
This was the wonder of the Lord- an unparallel example in the history of mankind.

Mian Mir asked, why was he enduring the suffering at the hands of his vile sinners when he possesseth superpowers? The Guru replied, "I **bear all this torture to set an example to the Teachers of True Name, that they may not lose patience or rail at God in affliction. The true test of faith is the hour of misery. Without examples to guide them, ordinary persons' minds quail in the midst of suffering."** Upon this Mian Mir departed commending the Guru's fortitude and singing his praises.

The Guru asked for a bath in Ravi river which flowed embracing the walls of Lahore city. Chandu reveled at the thought that the Guru's body full of blisters, would undergo greater pain when dipped in cold water and he permitted him to bathe in the river. The soldiers were sent to escort the Guru. The Master's disciples saw him leaving. He looked at them still forbidding any action. He said, "Such is the Will of my God, submit to the Divine Will, move not, stand calm against all woes."

Crowds watched the Master standing in water and having a dip. **Lo! The light blended with Light and the body was found nowhere. Hail to the Master! Thou art Wonderful- Martyr, the greatest. Thou art the Greatest!**

WE SALUTE THE MIGHTY KING!

This was the fourth day of the light half of the month of Jeth, Sambat 1663 (May 30, 1606 A.D.).

The doctrine of Bhana is the acceptance of the Will of God which is the core of Sikh faith. An enlightened mind lives according to inner dictates of His Hukam (order). It is a dedicated submission and infinite patience to accept His Will. **Guru Arjan sowed the seed of martyrdom which largely flourished after him and became the heritage of the Sikhs.**

GURU HAR GOBIND
(1595-1644, Guruship 1606-1644)

AKAL TAKHAT:

The martyrdom of Guru Arjan was an unparallel act in the history of mankind. The Guru had all the superpowers. He could have averted the situation in any way he liked, but he went through all that torture to show to the world how in all thick and thin one should cheerfully submit to the sweet Will of God.

As a matter of fact, the contents of the Adi Granth were not meant for the Yogis, Sidhas, Sanyasis nor for the Muslim Suffis only, who sit in seclusion in the caves of the Himalayas and worship the Almighty by denouncing the world. Instead the teachings of the Adi Granth were meant for the family men. By leading the family life, the Gurus gave practical examples as how to live according to Guru's Word.

The cruel and torturous execution of Guru Arjan aroused a very strong wave of angry feelings among the masses. The enlightened, but not passive, sufferings of the Guru instilled a new spirit and life into the people and they resolved to exert and sacrifice themselves for the sake of righteousness. For centuries, countless Hindu men, women and children had fallen under the Muslim sword and this did not soften the stone hearts of their oppressors; but rather they had become more cruel and brutal. Sometimes it is possible to reform the evil doer by opposing untruth and injustice through non-violent methods. The silent resistance and suffering for righteous cause might sometimes enable the tyrant to see his evil actions and he can be improved. But history stands witness that no amount of non-violence can succeed against a tyrant who is hardened and steeped in criminal oppressive ways and who pays no heed to basic values of moral and civilized conduct. Against such men, non-violence is only another name of disgraceful cowardice in their dictionary. Such power drunk men must be faced bravely with a stick bigger than theirs.

The Guru issued an order to the Masands (leaders of his followers) that he would be pleased with those who brought offerings of arms and horses instead of money. He laid down the foundation of Akal Takhat (Timeless Throne) in 1606 (the fifth day of light half of month of Har, Sambat 1663) just in front of Hari Mandar, and it was completed in 1609. Akal Takhat was built of solid bricks on a raised platform of about ten feet in height and looked like a throne. The Guru took his seat on it. He built Akal Takhat a few yards in front of Hari Mandar with a view that a Sikh at Akal Takhat should not forget that spiritual elevation was as essential as his social obligations. As a matter of fact, the Guru wanted his followers to be 'saint-soldiers', extremely cultured, highly moral with spiritual height and be ever-ready to measure swords with demoniac forces.

Akal Takhat grew into an institution which symbolized in itself the idea that the use of sword for the protection of righteousness and for self-defense was called for. Here the Guru sitting on his throne, would watch wrestling bouts and military feats of his disciples performed in the open arena opposite to the Akal Takhat. As all intricate cases and disputes were finally decided here by the Guru, the Akal Takhat served the purpose of a Supreme Court for the Sikhs. Besides throne, the Guru adopted all other emblems of royalty- the umbrella, the swords, the crest and the hawk, and thus the Sikhs called him a true king or 'Sacha Padshah'- a king in all appearance but in deeds and in purity as holy and great as previous Gurus. People looked towards Akal Takhat for guidance in their secular affairs. This custom became so significant that the decision once taken at Akal Takhat was followed by the Sikhs enthusiastically and this was the reason that they were always able to overcome every peril. The development of this custom contributed a lot towards the consolidation of the Sikh Movement. Akal Takhat is the highest seat of Sikh Religion today.

GURU HAR RAI
(1630-1661, Guruship 1644-1661)

GURU HAR KRISHEN
(1656-1664, Guruship 1661-1664)

GURU TEGH BAHADUR
(1621-1675, Guruship 1664-1675)

MARTYRDOM OF GURU TEGH BAHADUR:

As Mughal Emperor Aurangzeb ascended the throne of India by imprisoning his father and murdering his brothers, he decided to enlist the sympathies of the fanatical section of his co-religionists. His idea was to exterminate the idolatrous Hindus and to convert the whole of India to Islam. In order to achieve this objective he first tried peaceful overtures; secondly he offered money; thirdly he threatened punishment and lastly he tried to cause dissention among them. When all these measures failed, he resorted to forcible conversion. Orders were issued to the governors of all the provinces that they should destroy the schools and temples of the infidels and thereby put an end to educational activities as well as the practices of the religion of the Kafirs (non-Muslims meant Hindus).

The proselytizing zeal of the officials, with their campaign of religious persecution and their conversion at the point of the sword, had sent the wave of terror throughout the country. Sher Afghan Khan, the Emperor's viceroy in Kashmir, set about converting the Kashmiri Hindus by force and massacred those who opposed to embrace Islam. Even the Mohammadans who in any way assisted the Hindus, were mercilessly put to death. In extreme agony of too much slaughter, the Brahmin priests of Kashmir prayed to their gods. It is said that the Kashmiri Brahmins heard a supernatural voice who told them," Guru Nanak is the spiritual king in this age. Guru Tegh Bahadur is now seated on his throne. Go to him, he will protect your honor and your religion."

A deputation of Kashmiri Pandits (Brahmins) led by Pandit Kirpa Ram came to Anandpur and among tears of agony, they narrated their tales of woe and suffering to the Master. The Guru's eight years old son (Gobind Rai) appeared on the scene and asked his father why those people had tears in their eyes. He replied," The Emperor of India is converting the Hindus to Islam at the point of the sword and thus there is no end to the misery of these people."

"What is the remedy, father?" asked the son.

The Guru replied," This requires sacrifice- sacrifice of a holy and supreme soul." His son responded," O dear father, who is more holy than you in this age? Go and offer yourself and save these people and their religion." On hearing this the Guru asked the Kashmiri Brahmins to go to the Emperor and make the following representation to him," Guru Tegh Bahadur, the ninth Sikh Guru is now seated on the throne of the great Guru Nanak, who is the protector of faith and religion. First make him a Musalman and then all the people, including ourselves, will of our own accord adopt the faith of Islam."

Upon this the Brahmins went to Delhi and conveyed Guru's message to the Emperor who sent for the Guru. The Guru reached Delhi after long journey. There were three Sikhs, Bhai Mati Das, Bhai Dayala and

Bhai Sati Das with the Guru (Some writers account for five Sikhs- Mati Das, Gurditta, Uda, Chima and Dayala).

The Emperor explained that God appeared to him in a vision and told him to convert the whole world to Islam. Those who were to embrace Islam, would be rewarded with wealth, appointments, land revenue grants and lands. The Emperor tried to lure him," In this way you will have many disciples, and you will become a great priest of Islam. Therefore accept my religion- Islam, and you will receive from me whatever your heart may desire."

Guru showed the Emperor that instead of reducing the two religions to one, God wishes to make three religions out of two. So there shall be three religions- Hinduism, Islam, and Sikhism in the future. Upon this it was ordered that the Guru be imprisoned with sufficient guards around him. Again he was sent for and was told that if he embraced Islam, every service would be performed for him otherwise he would be severely tortured. He replied that he would never embrace Islam and thus, remained in Delhi jail for eight days. He was given three choices: firstly to embrace Islam; secondly to perform a miracle; and thirdly to prepare himself to court death. The Guru responded that to show a miracle was against the Will of God and thus he would not consent to the Emperor's proposals and the Emperor might act as he pleased. He was then put to extreme tortures.

Bhai Mati Das was bound between two pillars when the executioners put saw on his head, he began to recite Japji (the first Bani in Guru Granth Sahib)[1]. It is said that when his body was cut into two, he continued reciting Japji and he was silent only when the recitation of Japji was complete This was a wonder of Guru's Grace. Bhai Dayala was boiled to death in a cauldron of hot water. It is said that the third companion Bhai Sati Das was roasted alive with cotton wrapped round his body. The authorities thought that these tortures of his Sikhs might shake the

1. Japji is the first composition starting from page one of Guru Granth Sahib comprising of 38 pauris (stanzas) and a slok

Guru. Nothing could and nothing can shake the Divine Light (the Guru). The final message was given to the Guru, "You are to accept the religion of Islam or show a miracle. If you work a miracle, you may remain a Guru. If you accept Islam, then you will be advanced to an exalted position. If you fail to accept these offers, you shall be put to death. This is the final decision."

The Guru emphasized, "I will never abandon my faith. I want no honor in this life; I want honor hereafter. The threat of death possesses no terrors for me. For death I am prepared and I cheerfully accept it."

Hearing this reply it was ordered that the Guru should be executed. Saiyid Adam Shah accompanied by courtiers and Muslim priests came with a warrant for his execution. Many people turned out to witness the execution. He was then taken out of his cage and allowed to perform his ablutions. He sat under the banyan-tree where he recited Japji. The executioner, Jalal-ud-din of Samana (some say it was Adam Shah) took his sword and in a split of second, severed Guru's head from his body. This happened on the afternoon of Thursday, the fifth day of the month of Maghar in Sambat 1732 (November 11, 1675) at Chandni Chowk, Delhi where now stands Gurdwara Sis Ganj in his memory. History has recorded that a furious storm raged immediately after this brutal deed which filled every one's eyes with dust. Bhai Jaita dashed out of the crowd and instantaneously took away the holy head of the Guru to Anandpur (Punjab). He reached Kiratpur on the 15th of November, 1675. From there the Guru's head was taken to Anandpur with full honor and on the 16th of November, 1675, it was cremated with full ceremonies There is a Gurdwara called Sis Ganj at Anandpur where the hallowed head of the Guru was cremated.

Lakhi Shah Labana was a famous contractor in Delhi and he was also a follower of the Guru. He emptied his carts laden with lime near the Red Fort, taking advantage of the darkness and the carelessness of the Mughal sentries, and with the help of his sons, Nagahiya, Hema, Harhi and his friend Dhuma, whisked away the sacred body of the Guru, in one of their carts. Apprehensive of the government reprisal, Lakhi Shah and his sons then built up a pyre inside their own house and set fire to it. When the body was duly reduced to ashes, they cried out that their house had caught fire and called upon their neighbors to assist them in extinguishing it. Next day they collected the Guru's remains and buried them in a copper vessel called 'gaggar' in the earth under his funeral pyre. On this spot there stands a Gurdwara, Rakab Ganj, near Parliament House in New Delhi.

"Having broken his potsherd on the head of the king of
        Delhi, he departed for Paradise;
No one else coming into the world acted like Tegh Bahadur.

The world was in mourning for the departure of Tegh Bahadur;

There was weeping for him in the whole world, but rejoicing
        in paradise."

                          (Guru Gobind Singh- Bachitar Natak)

GURU GOBIND SINGH
(1666-1708, Guruship 1675-1708)

It may not be out of the way to say here that throughout the annals of human history, there was no other individual who could be of more inspiring personality than Guru Gobind Singh. At its climax the tenth Gur Nanak infused the spirit of both the saintlihood and the undauntedness in the minds and hearts of his followers to fight oppression in order to restore justice, righteousness (Dharma) and to uplift the down-trodden people in this world. It is said that after the martyrdom of Guru Tegh Bahadur, the tenth Master declared that he would create such a Panth (nation) which would not be cowed down by tyrant rulers but it would rather challenge the oppressor in every walk of life to restore justice, equality and peace for mankind. He further resolved that he would feel worthy to be called Gobind Singh only when any single member of his Khalsa Panth would successfully and undauntedly challenge the army of one hundred and twenty-five thousand opponents in the field. This point was rightfully proven at Chamkaur Sahib when Sahibzada Ajit Singh (Guru's about 18 years old eldest son) challenged the Mughal forces and their allies, the hilly Rajas.

"The Divine Guru hath sent me for religion's sake
On this account, I have come into the world;
Extend the faith everywhere
Seize and destroy the evil and sinful.
Understand this, ye holymen, in your minds
I assumed birth for the purpose of spreading the faith,
    saving the saints and extirpating all tyrants."
(Guru Gobind Singh- Chaupai, Bachitar Natak)

Guru Tegh Bahadur's martyrdom symbolized in itself the resistance to the tyranny of Muslim rule in favor of a new society. When evil is holding its head high, should a holy man knuckle under it or take up arms to combat and destroy it? The young Guru, Gobind Rai, decided in favor of the latter course i.e. to combat evil and uphold righteousness. He thus enjoined upon his followers to make use of the sword if all other means failed to liquidate the wicked and his wickedness. In order to achieve this mission, he issued 'Hukamnamas' (circular letters of authority) to his followers to present to him arms of different designs. The Guru's orders were obeyed with great zeal and devotion. He himself wore uniform and bore arms and induced others to practise archery and musket-shooting. He encouraged various muscle-developing and strenuous sports as part of the program of physical culture.

CREATION OF THE KHALSA:

The Guru sent Hukamnamas to his followers all over the country to visit Anandpur at the Baisakhi festival to be held in Sambat 1756 (13th April, 1699 A.D.). It seemed as if the whole of Punjab was on the move; and they came from all parts of the country.

A small tent was pitched on a small hill now called Kesgarh Sahib at Anandpur and an open air dewan (assembly) was held. **The Guru drew his sword and in a thundering voice said," I want one head, is there any one who can offer me?"** This most unusual call caused some terror in the gathering and the people were stunned. There was dead silence. The Guru made a second call. Nobody came forward. There was still more silence. On the third call there rose **Daya Ram, a khatri of Lahore who said," O true king, my head is at thy service."** The Guru took Daya Ram by the arm and led him inside the tent. A blow and thud were heard. Then the Guru, with his sword dripping with blood, came out and said," I want another head, is there anyone who can offer?"

Again on third call Dharam Das, a Jat from Delhi came forward and said," O true king! My head is at thy disposal." The Guru took Dharam Das inside the tent, again a blow and thud were heard, and he came out with his sword dripping with blood and repeated," I want another head, is there any beloved Sikh who can offer it?"

Upon this some people in the assembly remarked that the Guru had lost all reason and they went to his mother to complain. Mohkam Chand, a washerman of Dwarka (west coast of India) offered himself as a sacrifice. The Guru took him inside the tent and went through the same process. When he came out, he made a call for the fourth head. The Sikhs began to think that he was going to kill all of them. Some of them ran away and the others hung their heads down. Himmat Chand, a cook of Jagan Nath Puri, offered himself as a fourth sacrifice. Then the Guru made a fifth and the last call for a fifth head. Sahib Chand, a barber of Bidar (in central India), came forward and the Guru took him inside the tent. A blow and thud were heard.

The last time he stayed longer in the tent. People outside began to breath with relief. Inside the tent the Guru dressed them in splendid garments. They offered their heads to the Guru, and the Guru had now given them himself and his glory. When they were brought outside, they were in the most radiant form. There were exclamations of wonder and the sighs of regret on all sides. Now people were sorry for not offering their heads.

Since the time of Guru Nanak, Charanpauhal (baptism) had been customary form of initiation. People were to drink the holy water which had been touched or washed by the Guru's toe or feet. The Guru proceeded to initiate them to his new order by asking five faithful Sikhs to stand up. He put pure water into an iron vessel or Bowl (Batta of Sarbloh) and stirred it with a Khanda (two edged small sword). While stirring the water with Khanda, he recited Gurbani or Divine Word (Five Banis-Japji, Jap Sahib, Anand Sahib, Swayas, and Chaupai). Sugar crystals called 'Patasas' which incidentally the Guru's wife, Mata Sahib Kaur, had brought at that moment, were mixed in the water.

The Guru then stood up with the sacred Amrit (nectar) prepared in the steel bowl. Each of the five faithfuls, by turn, kneeling upon his left knee, looked up to the Master to receive his Eternal Light. He gave five palmfuls of Amrit to each of them to drink and sprinkled it five times in the eyes, asking them to repeat aloud with each sprinkle, "Waheguru ji ka Khalsa, Waheguru ji ki Fateh." (This meant: Khalsa belongs to God and all triumph be to His Name) Then he anointed them with five sprinkles in their head. In this way Amrit was administered to the five faithfuls from the same bowl. After that he asked them to sip Amrit from the same bowl to signify their initiation into **the casteless fraternity of the Khalsa. All the five faithfuls were baptized in this way by the Guru who then called them 'PANJ PYARAY' or Five Beloved Ones. He gave them the appellation of SINGHS or lions** and they were named from Daya Ram to Daya Singh, Dharam Das to Dharam Singh, Mohkam Chand to Mohkam Singh, Himmat Chand to Himmat Singh, and Sahib Chand to Sahib Singh. **The Guru then addressed them as the supreme, the liberated ones, pure ones and he called them THE KHALSA.**

He then ordained them to do the following:

I. First they must wear the following articles whose names begin with 'K':

1. Kes- not to cut hair(unshorn hair). This represents the natural appearance of saintlihood. This is the first token of Sikh faith.
2. Kanga- A comb to clean the hair.
3. Kachha- An underwear to denote chastity (a warrior's shorts).
4. Kara- A steel bracelet on the wrist, a symbol of dedication to the Guru.
5. Kirpan- A sword for self-defense and a symbol of dignity, power and unconquerable spirit.

II. They must observe the following guidelines:

1. Not to remove hair from the body.
2. Not to use Tobacco or other intoxicants.
3. Not to eat 'Kutha', a meat of an animal slaughtered by slow degrees as done by the Muslims.
4. Not to commit adultery- 'Par nari ki sej, bhul supne hun na jayo' (never enjoy, even in dream, the bed of a woman other than your own wife)
   (A supplementary ordinance was issued that any one who did not observe any of the four directives, must be re-baptized, pay a fine, and promise not to offend any more; or he must be excommunicated from the Khalsa).

III. They must rise at dawn, bathe, meditate on Gurmantar- 'Waheguru', Moolmantar- the preamble of Japji, and recite five banis- Japji, Jap Sahib and Swayas in the morning; Rehras in the evening; and Sohela at bed time at night.

IV. They must not have matrimonial relations with smokers, with persons who killed their daughters, with the descendants or followers of Prithi Chand, Dhir Mal, Ram Rai, or masands who had strayed away from the tenets and principles of Guru Nanak.

V. They must not worship idols, cemeteries, or cremation grounds, and must believe only in One Immortal God.

The Guru further spelled out that they should practice arms,and never show their backs to the foe in the battle field. They should always be ready to help the poor and protect those who sought their protection. They were to consider their previous castes erased, and deem themselves all brothers of one family. Sikhs were to intermarry among themselves.

THE MASTER BECOMES THE DISCIPLE:

After the Guru had administered Amrit to his Five Beloved Ones, he stood up in supplication and with folded hands, begged them to baptize him in the same way as he had baptized them. **This was the height of this remarkable episode setting up unparallel example in the world that first as Guru, he created the Khalsa blessing them with power, supremacy and glory, and then he himself became their disciple-Wonderful is Guru Gobind Singh, himself the Master and himself the disciple.** In the annals of human history a disciple could become a Guru but never a Guru became a disciple.

The Five Beloved Ones were astonished at such a proposal, and represented their own unworthiness, and the greatness of the Guru, whom they deemed God's Vicar upon earth.

Accordingly the Five Beloved Ones baptized the Guru with the same ceremonies and injunctions he himself had employed. The Guru was then named Gobind Singh instead of Gobind Rai.

Guru Gobind Singh was the first one to take Amrit from the Khalsa, the Five Beloved Ones. About 80,000 men and women were baptized within a few days at Anandpur.

By creating the Khalsa, the Guru embedded two qualities in one person. A Khalsa is a Saint-Soldier. A Sikh is a saint because he worships the All-Pervading Divine Spirit and in whom that Spirit shines day and night like a full moon. A Sikh is a soldier because he is ever ready to take up the arms to uphold righteousness.

With the creation of the Khalsa, some new doctrines were also established. The first doctrine of the Khalsa was the doctrine of the theocratic democracy by his selected, not elected, five representatives of the people from amongst the thousands of the devotees from all over the country while second was the doctrine of collective responsibility by authorizing the Five Beloved Ones only, in the presence of the holy Guru Granth Sahib to assume authority implicitly to be obeyed by the whole nation.

The Guru set the souls of the Khalsa free and filled their hearts with a lofty longing for religious and social freedom and national ascendancy. The Khalsa, therefore, accepted the challenge to combat terror inspired by tyranny of the powerful Mughal empire and embarked upon a national struggle of liberation.

After the creation of the Khalsa the hilly Rajas were alarmed at the Guru's increasing influence to convert crowds of Hindus and Muslims to join the ranks of the Khalsa. Some of the hilly Rajas approached the Emperor for protection and security of their rule.

Apart from small skirmishes between the Khalsa army and the hilly Rajas, there were at least five major battles between the armies of the Guru and that of hilly Rajas and the Emperor. Ultimately the Emperor requested the Guru to leave Anandpur and promised safe passage.

At last the Guru left Anandpur on December 20-21, 1705. The moment the enemy got the news of Guru's departure, they again forgot all about their pledges and set out in hot pursuit immediately.

After crossing the overflowing Sarsa river, Guru's family was scattered. At the famous battle of Chamkaur, Guru's two eldest sons (18 years and 14 years old) fell fighting the imperial army and the armies of hilly Rajas and others. Guru's two younger sons (7 years and 9 years old) were executed while bricking them alive in the wall at Sirhind by the Imperial Governor.

The Guru stayed at Dina for some days. It was here that he **wrote his celebrated 'Zafarnama'**, or Persian epistle to Emperor Aurangzeb. It was in fact an exquisite reply to the letters of the invitation to the Guru which he had received from the Emperor. The letter is characteristic of the sublimity of the Guru and each line is pregnant with stimulating truths and righteous indignation. He wrote to the Emperor that he had no faith in his solemn promises in the name of God and oaths on the Quran. The fact remained that he, the Emperor, on all occasions violated his sacred promises and proved false, mean and treacherous. The Guru wrote,"......What though my four sons were killed, I remain behind like a coiled snake. What bravery is it to quench a few sparks of life? Thou art merely exciting a raging fire the more...........As thou didst forget thy word on that day, so will God forget thee.

God will grant thee the fruit of the evil deed thou didst design......Thou art proud of thine empire, While I am proud of the kingdom of the Immortal God.........When God is a friend, what can an enemy do even though he multiply himself a hundred times? If an enemy practice enmity a thousand times, he cannot, as long as God is a friend, injure even a hair of one's head."

The letter was sent through Bhai Daya Singh and Dharam Singh to the Emperor and they delivered it to him in Daccan. This letter awakened the Emperor's dormant conscience and evoked in him a sense of true repentance. It cast such a miracle effect on him that he began to pine and soon confined to bed. Aurangzeb dictated this letter to his son when death was at hand, in which he acknowledged his defeat in the life that he led:

"......Whatever good or bad I have done, I am taking it as a load upon my head to the Great Unseen............I am totally in the dark about the destiny that awaits me. But what I know is that I have committed enormous sins. Canst tell what grim punishment is in the store for me........."

GURU AT DAMDAMA SAHIB:

By this time all restrictions against the Guru by the Mughal government had been removed. On receipt of Zafarnama, the governors had been ordered by Aurangzeb to cease all molesting activities against him. It was here that the Guru's wife joined him. When she arrived, he was seated in a big gathering of his disciples. Addressing the Master, she asked,

"Where are my four sons?"
The Master replied,
"What then if thy four are gone?
They yet live, and shall ever live- the Khalsa,
Millions of our dear brave sons."
The Master sent for the Adi Granth from Kartarpur, near Beas, in order to incorporate Guru Tegh Bahadur's hymns in it. The original copy was with the Dhirmalias and they refused to part with it and rather remarked that if Guru Gobind Singh was the Guru, he should make one himself. **It was here that Guru Gobind Singh dictated the whole of Granth Sahib as it stands today, to Bhai Mani Singh.**

This sacred volume is called 'Damdama Sahib di Bir'. This Bir was installed at Hari Mandar Sahib but it is not available NOW. It is not known whether it has been destroyed or taken away by Ahmed Shah Abdali when he plundered the town of Amritsar during one of his raids.

GURU AT NADER (DECCAN):

When it was clear to him that the call of the Father from Heaven had come, he gave his last and enduring message of his mission to the assembly of the Khalsa. On Wednesday, October 6, 1708 (on Budhwar, Katik Chauth, Shukla Pakkh, samvat 1765) at Nander (Deccan), he asked Bhai Daya Singh to bring Sri Granth Sahib. **He then opened the Granth Sahib, placed five paise and a coco-nut before it and solemnly bowed**

to it as his SUCCESSOR, GURU GRANTH SAHIB. Saying 'Waheguru ji ka Khalsa, Waheguru ji ki Fateh', he circumambulated the sacred volume and proclaimed," O beloved Khalsa, let him who desireth to behold me, behold the Guru Granth. Obey the Granth Sahib. It is the visible body of the Gurus. And let him who desireth to meet me, diligently search its hymns." He then sang his self-composed hymn:

"Agya bhai Akal ki tabhi chalayo Panth
Sabh Sikhan ko hukam hai Guru manyo Granth
Guru Granth Ji manyo pargat Guran ki deh
Jo Prabhu ko milbo chahe khoj shabad mein le."

Translation of the above:

"Under orders of the Immortal Being, the Panth was created.
All the Sikhs are enjoined to accept the Granth as their Guru.
Consider the Guru Granth as embodiment of the Gurus.
Those who want to meet God, can find Him in its hymns."

The above ceremony is described in Bhatt Vahi Bhadson Parganah Thanesar (one of the writtings of Bhatts) as:

"Guru Gobind Singhji, mahal daswan, beta Guru Tegh
Bahadurji ka, pota Guru Hargobindji ka, parpota Guru
Arjanji ka, bans Guru Ramdasji ki, Surajbansi, Gosal gotra,
Sodhi Khatri, basi Anandpur, parganah Kahlur, muqam Nander,
tad Godavari, des Dakkhan, sammat satran sai painsath, kartik
mas ki chauth, shukla pakkhe, budhwar ke dihn, Bhai Daya Singh
se bachan hoya, Sri Granth Sahib lai ao, bachan pai Daya Singh
Sri Granth Sahib lai aye; Guruji ne panch paise ek narial aagey
bheta rakha, matha teka, sarbatt sangat se kaha, mera hukam
hai, meri jagah Sri Granthji ko janana, jo sikh janega tis ki
ghal thaen paegi, Guru tis ki bahuri karega, satt kar manana."

Translation of the above:

"Guru Gobind Singh, the Tenth Master, son of Guru Tegh
Bahdur, grandson of Guru Hargobind, great-grandson of
Guru Arjan, of the family of Guru Ram Das, Surajbansi
Gosal clan, Sodhi Khatri, resident of Anandpur, parganah
Kahlur, now at Nander, in the Godavari country in Deccan,
asked Bhai Daya Singh, on Wednesday, Katik chauth,
shukla pakkh, samvat 1765 (October 6, 1708) to bring
Sri Granth Sahib. In obedience to his orders, Daya Singh
brought the Granth Sahib. The Guru placed before it five paise
and a coconut and bowed his head before it. He then said to
the sangat (holy gathering), "It is my commandment: Own Sri
Granthji in my place. He who so acknowledges, will obtain
his reward. The Guru will rescue him. Know this as the truth."

He then left for his heavenly abode. The Sikhs made preparations for his
final rites as he had instructed them, the Sohila was chanted and Parsahd
(sacred food) was distributed. While all were mourning the loss, a Sikh
arrived and said," You suppose that the Guru is dead. I met him this very
morning riding his bay horse. After bowing to him when I asked whither
he was going, he smiled and replied that he was going to the forest on a
hunting excursion."

The Sikhs who heard this statement arrived at the conclusion that
**it was all the Guru's play, that he dwelt in uninterrupted bliss, that
he showed himself wherever he was remembered. He who trea-
sures even a grain of the Lord's love in his heart, is the blessed
one and the Guru reveals himself to such a devotee in mysterious
ways.** Therefore, for such a Guru who had departed bodily to Heaven,
there ought to be no mourning.

The Master returned to his Eternal Home on the 5th of the bright
half of Katik, Sambat 1765 (7th October, 1708 A.D.). He was 42 years
of age.

Before leaving this world, the Guru had ordained," If any one erects a shrine in my honor, his offspring shall perish."

The Sikh temple at Nader is called Abchalnagar. It was built by Maharaja Ranjit Singh in 1832 in defiance of the Guru's interdiction. After Maharaja Ranjit Singh, the rule of his dynasty, therefore, came to an end. Guru's prophecy was fulfilled.

GURU GRANTH SAHIB
(1708 - For Ever)

DIVINE WORD CAME DIRECT FROM GOD:

Guru Granth Sahib does not narrate the life story of Guru Nanak, but each and every word is dedicated to the Glory of the Almighty God only. It is not a blend or reproduction of earlier religions, but the Divine Word (Gurbani) came to the Gurus direct from God. Guru Nanak stated that it was not his philosophy neither it was his understanding nor it was his thinking, but the Word was coming to him direct from God and he was simply delivering His message to the world. As he confirms:

'O Lalo*, as comes the Divine Word from Lord to me,
    So do I narrate it.'
                (Tilang Mohalla 1, p-722 Guru Granth Sahib)
        (*Lalo was Guru's disciple).

'I have said what Thou
    commandeth me to say.'
                (Wadhans Mohalla 1,p-566)

This was repeatedly confirmed and emphasized by all the Gurus. The tenth Master, Guru Gobind Singh ended the personal Guruship and conferred Guruship upon the Adi Granth (the Sikh Holy Scripture- the

Divine Word) and then bowed before it declaring it as the Last Guru for ever (Present as well as future Guru). When the Guruship was passed on, the Adi Granth was called Guru Granth Sahib which too became the embodiment of Divine Light. It should, therefore, be remembered very clearly that bowing before Guru Granth Sahib as Sikhs do, **is not bowing before a book, but it is a bowing before the Divine Light or JOT (Guru) which was passed on by the Guru when the Guruship was conferred upon it.**

GURU GRANTH SAHIB BEGINS UNIQUELY:

In Hindu mythology the word 'OM' always meant for God as monotheistic. Then they started interpreting it as more than one God. Guru Nanak put an integer '1' before it and a kar (a semi-circle) after it. Thus it becomes 'EK-OM-KAR' and by doing so, he sealed the position for ever meaning **'There is One and only One God'**. Therefore Guru Granth Sahib uniquely begins with numeral One ('1'). The One Absolute is the monotheistic conception of God and is represented by numerical symbol here. One God does not only mean numerically one but Unique without a second like Him.

Guru Granth Sahib begins with Mool-Mantar or the Preamble of Japji which is the Essence of the whole Guru Granth Sahib:

੧ ੴ ਸਤਿਨਾਮੁ ਕਰਤਾ ਪੁਰਖੁ ਨਿਰਭਉ ਨਿਰਵੈਰੁ
ਅਕਾਲ ਮੂਰਤਿ ਅਜੂਨੀ ਸੈ ਭੰ ਗੁਰਪ੍ਰਸਾਦਿ ॥

Ek-Onm-Kaar   There is But One God
Sat-Naam   He is the Eternal Truth

Karta-Purkh	Almighty Creator
Nirbhao-Nirvair	Unfearful, Without hate and enmity
Akaal-Murat	Immortal Entity
Ajuni, Saibhang	Unborn, Self-Existent
Gurparsaad	Realized by the Grace of True Guru

The next verse is generally called Sach (True) Mantar:

Jap   Meditate upon
Aad Sach - Who was True before the Creation
Jugad Sach - Who was True in the beginning of Creation
Haibhi Sach - Who is True now, and O Nanak
Nanak Hosibhi Sach - Who shall be True for ever.

Guru Granth Sahib is the only savior of human beings thrown in the violent sea of this worldly life. It helps a person to live by certain directives or moral codes which are necessary for the achievement of salvation of the soul.

Guru Granth Sahib signifies the importance of Naam (Name of God) by identifying it with the Guru. Naam releases an individual from all previous sins, sorrows, suffering and cycle of death and rebirth. **No rituals, no alms, no sacrifices, no fasts and no penances equal Naam.**

Guru Granth Sahib initiates a disciple on the path of spiritual progress and guides him at the various stages of his journey to God. **It is a ship that steers clear a devotee through the ocean of Maya (Materialism), thus, leading the human soul to its ultimate destination which is the Absolute Bliss.**

Guru Granth Sahib was written and compiled by the Gurus themselves and thus, is completely authentic and is preserved in its original form. It is the most valuable possession which Sikhs have received from

God through Guru Nanak and is held in supreme reverence by them.

Guru Granth Sahib is in poetic form composed in 31 Indian Classical Raagas (musical measures). In addition to 31 Raagas, there are Slokas, Vars and Swaiyias. There are 36 authors whose Bani (Word) is incorporated in it. It contains a total of 5,872 Hymns (Sabads or Stanzas) of which 4,956 Hymns belong to Six Sikh Gurus (first five and the ninth). The remaining Sabads belong to 15 Bhagats or saints (778 Hymns), four devout Sikhs (17 Hymns) and 11 Bhats or Minstrels (121 Swaiyias). These 30 saints belonged from the highest caste Brahmins to the lowest caste Sudras, and Muslims as well as Hindus. **Guru Granth Sahib is indeed a Universal Bible in the world which contains Divine Message not only for the Sikhs but for the entire Humanity.**

WHAT IS GOD?

   We have neither heard nor found any writing starting with a numeral. The Sikh Holy Scripture (Guru Granth Sahib) begins with numeral '1' indicating the Oneness of God and the fact that there is no Second like Him. Guru Granth Sahib begins with the Definition of God:

Ek-Onm-kaar	God is One but only One
Sat-Naam	Eternal Truth
Karta-Purkh	Almighty Creator
Nirbhao	Unfearful
Nirvair	Without hate and enmity
Akaal Murat	Immortal Entity
Ajuni	Unborn
Saibhang	Self-Existent
Gurparsaad	Realized by the Grace of True Guru (Divine Word)

This is called Mool-Mantar

Jap	Thou shall worship
Aad Sach	Who was True before the Creation
Jugaad Sach	Who was True in the beginning of Creation
Haibhi Sach	Who is True Now, and O Nanak
Nanak Hosibhi Sach	Who Shall be True For Ever

This is called Sach (True) Mantar.

   There are three tenses in the world - past, present and future but Guru Nanak used the fourth tense too and that is He was True before the Creation, in the beginning of the Creation, now and in the future for ever. The above (Mool-Mantar + Sach Mantar) is called the Preamble of Guru Granth Sahib. Some call it God while others call it Ram or Allah but Sikhism calls this Power as Waahay-Guru (Wonderful God).

Doctrine of God has been clearly revealed in the opening paragraph of Sikh Holy Scripture as being One and Only One. The Oneness of God does not only mean numerically one but Unique without a second like Him. He is the Absolute One. In Asa Mohalla 1, page 10 of Guru Granth Sahib, Guru Nanak says, "Such is His greatest merit that there is none like Him. Neither there was any other, nor shall there ever be like Him." Guru further describes Him in Japji Sahib(24), page 5 of Guru Granth Sahib::

> "Great is the Lord and High is His Mansion,
> Supreme above all is His Name.
> If only one is as exalted as He, might know His extent,
> But how great He is, only He Himself knows."

God is the defender of the right and chastiser of evil. He has no wants nor imperfections and hence His act of creation is not an ordinary act but it is a manifestation of His Eternal Power. The whole realm of existence , liberation and bondage all are created and governed by The Eternal Writ of God . God's Will is All-pervasive and Absolute. Every good that comes to human beings, is His gift. All virtues, excellences and perfections in individuals are due to His Grace. Guru Nanak made every effort to secure all praise, adoration, love and worship for the One and only One God. He condemned image worship and denounced idols. **There can be no image of the One Who is Formless.** Guru Nanak exhorts human beings that there should be ceaseless remembrance and contemplation of the Holy Name till the human soul becomes one with Him. In Sikh monotheistic concept of God, He is a symbol of perfection, not incarnated but self-existent and eternal. He is conceived as an object of veneration and reverence by the Sikhs.

Ek-On-Kaar:
The word Om (Om) was used for God and to write it in the beginning of

Granths (scriptures), letters and other writings. Guru Nanak put numeral '1' before Om meaning that there is One God and put 'Kar' after Om which means that there is One God and there is nothing else but Only One God. So Guru Nanak sealed this situation for ever saying 'Ek-On-Kar ' - God is One but Only One. Then he used Onkar (Onmkar) as Super Being Lord (God). So Onkar is He who created Brahma, who created mountains and Yugas (ages), who created Vedas and who emancipated all through Divine Word.

Guru Nanak went to Banaras (also called Varanasi in India) which was known as the seat of Hindu Religious Learning and abode of Shiva. Pandit Chatur Das was the chief Brahmin of the city. There was long discussion between the two. The Guru asked the Pundit what did he learn, what did he teach to the people and what type of knowledge did he impart to his disciples? The Pandit replied, "By the Will of God I teach fourteen sciences to the people." The Guru explained that better than all these sciences was the knowledge of God. Upon this the Guru uttered the fifty-four stanzas of Ramkali Mohalla 1- Dakhani Onmkar given at page 929 of Guru Granth Sahib.. The True God is superior to all other gods. On hearing the Sabad of Ramkali, Pandit Chatur Das fell at the feet of the Guru, and became his Sikh. He did a lot to spread Sikh Religion in that area. Some of those stanzas of Dakhni Onmkar are given below:

"Onkar is He who created Brahma
Onkar is He who fashioned the human mind.
Onkar is He who created mountains and Yugas (ages).
It is the One Lord (Onkar) who created Vedas.
Onkar is He who, through the Word, Emancipated all.
It is the One Supreme Lord through Whom God-men were saved.
Listen to discourse on the syllable Om[1] worthy of obeisance-
The Eternal Lord is the essence of three worlds." (1)
Hear, O Pandit[2], why writest thou the worldly puzzles?

1- The syllable Onum (Om Namo) used in teaching that is associated with Omkar (Onkar).
2- Hindu learned Brahmin.

By Guru's Grace, write thou only the Name of the Lord,
The Cherisher of the world. (Pause)
"God created the whole world spontaneously and
Permeated the three worlds[3] with His Light.
Pick up thou the gems and pearls of the Name and by the Guru's grace
Thou shall obtain God, the Real commodity.
If man understands, reflects and comprehends what he reads and pursues, he
Ultimately comes to realize the True Lord within All.
The pious person perceives and contemplates the True Lord,
Without the True One, this world is but Illusion. " (2)

"Loving another (than God) man loses Divine Knowledge, he
becomes rotten in ego and eats poison.
He who loves not the Lord's Praise, loses the Profound and
Unfathomable Lord.
But if one loves the Guru's True Utterance, one obtains Nectar
and mind and body in truth finds joy.
The Lord Himself is the Exalted Guru, Himself He blesses man
with Nectar-Name and Himself makes him drink this Nectar." (4)
"Everyone says, "He is One," but each is engrossed in ego and
pride.
But he who knows the One Lord within and without, he sees the
Lord's Presence in his very home.
The Lord is near: think Him not afar: He alone Permeates the
whole world.
There is but One Lord. There is not another, Nanak, remains
merged in One Lord. " (5)

3- One world is what is at our level to infinity.
   Second world is what is above us to infinity and
   Third world is what is below us to infinity.

"The One God is in all ways, all forms, all colors.
He works through air, water, fire and various shapes.
The One soul wanders through the three worlds.
And if one realizes the One Lord, one is blessed with honor.
He who gathers Divine wisdom and meditation, abides in the
state of Equipoise.
Some rare one attains to One Lord by Guru's grace.
He, who is blest by His Grace, he attains Bliss.
And he utters (the Truth) through the Guru's Word."   (7)

As a matter of fact the whole of Guru Granth Sahib is about the Concept of God. It is wholly dedicated to the Glory of the Almighty God Only. The Guru further elaborates the Concept of God in Rag Sorath:

"The Unseen, Infinite, Inaccessible, Inapprehensible God is not
subject to death or destiny.
He is of no caste, unborn, self-existent, without fear or doubt.
I am a sacrifice to the Truest of the True.
He hath no form or color or outline.
He becometh manifest by the True Word.
He hath no mother, father, son, or kinsman;
He feeleth no lust, and hath no wife or family;
He is Pure, endless, and infinite; all Light is Thine, O Lord.
God is concealed in every heart, His Light is in every heart.
He whose understanding's adamantine doors are opened by the
Guru's instruction, fixeth his gaze on the Fearless One.
God having created animals, made them subject to death, and
retained all contrivances in His Own power..
He who serveth the True Guru obtaineth the real boon, and is
delivered by repeating the Word.
Truth is contained in pure vessels; few there are whose acts are
pure.
By seeking Thy protection, saith Nanak, the soul blendeth with

the Supreme soul"
> (Sorath Moh. 1, p-597, Guru Granth Sahib)

(All quotations are from Guru Granth Sahib unless it is noted otherwise)

GOD - IMPERSONAL AND PERSONAL:

God is both Impersonal (Nirgun) and Personal (Sargun). Impersonal God is Formless beyond human reach. When He reveals Himself through His Creation, He becomes Personal and related. It is just like the rays coming from sun. The source is Formless and the whole universe is His Personal form. No form howsoever unique it may be, is independent of Him. Infinite can manifest into an unlimited number of finites but any number of finites, alone or together, cannot be equal to the Infinite. **So any finite form cannot be worshipped as God, Who is Infinite and Formless:**

> " God is Formless, colorless, markless,
> He is casteless, classless, creedless,
> His form, hue, shape and garb
> Cannot be described by anyone.
> He is the Spirit of Eternity,
> Self-Radiant, He shineth in His Splendor."
>> (Guru Gobind Singh)

God neither takes birth nor does He die:
> "Burnt be the tongue that says
> The Lord takes birth and undergoes death."
>> (Bhairon Moh. 5, p-1136)

GOD IS WITHOUT HATE AND ANIMOSITY:

God is not Revengeful but He is Gracious and beyond measure Merciful. He Himself never brings calamity to punish the people rather it is our own actions that bring disaster as punishment. As you sow so shall you reap. For example there are millions of people living in a city. All of them are not in the jail or all of them are not on death roll. Those who committed crime are the only ones who are in the jail. Those who murdered someone are the only ones who are on the death roll. The rest of the population is living happily and enjoying. Those who are in the jail or are on death roll, are not punished by the president but they are there because of their actions. How can any one blame the president for their punishment? In the same way God does not punish anyone, we are responsible for our actions. God is rather Gracious. Even a worst sinner in this world would be pardoned when surrenders before the Almighty. The Divine Word says:

> "The sinner who is patronless in the world, when surrenders
> before the Lord Gets deliverance."
>
> (Bhairon Moh. 5, p-1141)

There are so many examples in history to prove His Graciousness. It is recorded that Ajamal was an atheist. He was Brahmin by caste and was living with a prostitute. Being a Brahmin and living with a prostitute is a cardinal sin according to the eastern religions. She gave birth to a son who died immediately. History reveals that she gave birth to six sons and every one of them died immediately after birth. Ajamal was completely shaken up. He met a Sadhu (a blessed saint) and told his story of grief. The Sadhu suggested to Ajamal that if he meditated on the Name, the situation would change. But being an atheist Ajamal refused to do so. However he agreed at the end. The Sadhu told him to meditate on the Name, "Narayan (God)" and that he should focus his attention in the meaning of the Word and repeat, "Narayan, Narayan, Narayan ...." After some time again a son was born but this time he did not die. Ajamal was wonder-struck and named him, 'Narayan'. So whenever he called his son by name (Narayan), actually he was also meditating on the Name. Ajamal got salvation.

"For the love of his son Ajamal uttered 'Narayan'-

Who smote and drove away the Death's myrmidons."

(Maru Mohalla 5, p-999)

Guru Nanak is explaining that if a notorious and recognized sinner like Ajamal can get salvation by meditating on the Name, anybody can get deliverance if one surrenders to Him. The Essence of the Sikh Religion is the Meditation on the Name (of God). **Nam (Name) is the central theme in the House of Guru Nanak:**
"The Lord has given Nanak the gift of this game
That in his home Resounds only the Name."

(Bhairon Mohalla 5, p-1136)

The paramount Characteristic of God, Guru explains, is that whosoever surrenders to Him, gets Deliverance:
"God embraces him who seeketh His protection
This is the characteristic of the Lord."

(Bihagra Moh.5, p-544)

WHERE IS GOD?

After visiting Mecca and Madina, Guru Nanak went to Baghdad. There he met Behlol, a high Muslim priest. He told Guru Nanak," You have to answer our questions or we will punish you." Guru replied, "I do not answer questions under any kind of threat but I have set out from my home just to answer the questions of this world." Behlol addressed, "I have been worshiping Allah, I have been meditating but three questions are always hanging on my mind, pray if you kindly answer those questions:
First- What was before God?
Second- Where does God live?
Third- What does He do?"

Guru Nanak responded, "I will answer your first question only after you offer me pearls." Behlol brought pearls and offered them to him. The Guru then asked Behlol, "Please slowly but loudly start counting the pearls." Behlol started," One, two." Guru stopped him there saying that he was counting wrong. Start counting again slowly but loudly. Behlol started counting again," One, two, three……." Guru stopped Behlol again saying that he was still counting wrong and told him to try one more time and warned him that he would stop him if he committed the same mistake. Behlol started, "One." Guru one more time stopped him right there and asked ," Does counting begin with one?" **The Divine Guru cast one gracious glance towards Behlol who got the Realization.** Behlol said," Sir, I am not counting wrong. Nothing is before one and the counting begins only with one." This meant that nothing was before One (God). Behlol got the answer of his first question and touched Guru's feet in acknowledgement, "He is the competent and perfect Faqir (prophet)."

Before answering the second question the Guru said to Behlol, "I will answer your second question only after you offer me milk."

A bowl of milk was brought and offered to the Guru.

Guru looked at Behlol saying, "This milk is not pure, it has some mixture in it."

Behlol replied," Sir, the bowl was thoroughly cleaned and pure milk was poured in it. So it is pure."

The Guru again told him, "No, it is not pure."

The Guru then asked Behlol, "Does this milk have butter in it?"

Behlol replied, "Yes sir, it has butter in it."

The Guru then explained," The milk has butter in it but eyes cannot see it. In the same way the bowl of entire firmament has butter (God) in it but it is not seen." God is everywhere but cannot be seen.

At the end the Guru told Behlol that he would answer his remaining question only if he lets him sit in his seat. Behlol vacated his seat and let Guru sit in his place. While seated in Behlol's spot the Guru went into a trance. "Sir," asked Behlol, "You have not answered the third question, rather you are sitting motionless with your eyes closed." Guru Nanak opened his eyes and said, "Those who sit on the throne, God can bring them down and those who are sitting down, He can put them on the throne. This is what God does."

Behlol touched Guru's feet. After that whenever Guru Nanak wanted to leave, Behlol begged him to stay. According to Sikh history, the Guru stayed there for 17 days before he came back from Baghdad.

Behlol became Guru's follower. History narrates that he spent sixty long years meditating -sitting at the foot of the slab, where the sacred feet of the Guru had rested during their discussion. Later on a shrine was built on this spot in the memory of the Guru. The English translation of the inscription on the slab inside the shrine is:

> "In memory of the Guru, that is the Divine Master, Baba Nanak, Faqir Aulia, this building has been raised with the help of seven saints, and the chronogram reads. The blessed disciple has produced a spring of Grace year 917 (Muslim year)."
> (The Sikh Review- October-November 1969 (issue), p.113)

Swami Anand Acharya of Sweden mentions in his book, 'Snow Bird', published by Macmillan & Sons, London, that during his visit to Baghdad, he found another inscription on the slab dated 917 Hijri. The inscription reads:

> "Here spoke the Hindi Guru Nanak to Faqir Behlol, and for these sixty years since the Guru left Iraq, the soul of Behlol has rested on Master's word like a bee poised on a dawn-lit honey rose."

It is said that once Shah of Iran came to see Behlol and he was so much wonder-struck seeing the glow on his face that he remarked, "If the sight of your face is so wondrous and beauteous, what about your Guru (Nanak)?"

There is a Sikhs Gurdwara (Sikh church) in his memory on this spot where the sacred   feet of Guru Nanak rested during this discussion in Baghdad, Iraq.

GOD IS THE SAVIOR OF HIS SAINTS:

God is the one and the only one savior of the humanity but His devotees (saints) are particularly near and dear to Him. Harnakhash was the king of Multan (now in Pakistan) and an staunch atheist. He had a son, Prahlad who was a devotee of the Lord. He used to meditate on the Word, 'Ram' but his father (Harnakhash) did not like it and asked him not to do it. When Prahlad did not stop, his father would punish him. Prahlad's mother pleaded with his son, "My dear son, he is your father and he is also a king, so do what he tells you to do and do not meditate on the word, 'Ram' and save your life." Prahlad replied, "Mother, I will not stop reciting His name, my Guru has instructed me to do so." The Sikh Scripture describes the exchange between the mother and the son:

"The mother counseled the son, 'My dear son, abandon the Name of the Lord and save thy life.'

(But) said Prahlad, "Hark, O dear mother, I'll not abandon the Name of God, for, such is the instruction of my Guru."

(Bhairo Mohalla 3, p-1133)

His teachers complained to the king that his son had not only gone astray but he made his classmates gone astray too. Ultimately Harnakhash got one very thick iron rod and put it in the fire till it turned red hot. He then dared Prahlad to embrace it. When Prahlad went near the rod, he saw an ant moving on the rod. He thought to himself that if a small ant could crawl on the red hot iron bar, he could embrace it too. Wonder of the Lord! When Prahlad embraced the rod, he found it cold. The Divine Word says:

"The devotee Prahlad was protected

And Harnakhash was torn apart with claws[4]"

(Maru Mohalla 5, p-999)

The love of God gave Prahlad courage and fearlessness and he asked for divine intervention. God protected him in distress and saved him in a miraculous way. For the sake of His devotee, the supreme Lord assumed a different form and emerged out of the pillar tearing Harnakhash apart. Such miracles and supernatural help of God are considered a proof of His deep love for His saints. To protect His devotees is God's paramount characteristic (Birdh). Practice of praising the Glory of the Lord is the highest of all practices. Sikh history proves that reciting His Name in all awareness saves His devotees from dangers. The story of Prahlad and autobiographic statements of Namdev and Kabir show that when in crisis, they prayed for help, God intervened and saved them. Saints and devotees in all ages have prayed to Him during their time of need and got divine help.

These supernatural miracles of God should be distinguished from the miracles of the human beings which are performed by their magical powers. Miracles performed by Sidhas and Yogis were different from divine interventions. Supernatural and miraculous actions performed by His Might are deemed as part of His doctrine for the preservation of higher values. It is a concept of Divine Justice overtaking evil deeds. God shows miracles to protect the righteous while other powers shown by human beings with magic are against the Will of God and are considered to be dangerous. He protects His saints and prophets from perils and pitfalls unless He wills that their suffering and martyrdom should serve a higher purpose.

"In every age God created His Devotees and preserved their honor.
The wicked Harnakhash was slain and Prahlad was protected.
On the egotists and slanderers the Lord turned His back and

4- It is said that Narsingh (who is half man and half lion) came and tore apart Harnakhash with his nails.

Namdev[5] He ushered into His Presence.
Nanak has contemplated such a Lord (God) Who Emancipates
   him in the end."

(Asa Mohalla 4, p-451)

God is not under anybody. He is not swayed by anyone. He does not yield to any power. But He is ever pleasing by the devotion of His Devotees:

"One gains (pleases) Thee not, O God, by despising the world.
Nor, if one reads the Vedas.
Nor, if one bathes in pilgrim-stations,
Nor, if one roams the whole world through.
Nor, by being knowledgeable and clever.
Nor, if one gives away more and more in charity.
For, everyone is under Thy Sway, O Inaccessible and
Inapprehensible God.
But, Thou art in the power (of devotion) of Thy Devotees
   And they lean on Thee alone."

(Ramkali ki Var- Moh.5, Pauri, p-962)

GOD IS THE CHERISHER:

"My tongue utters solely Thy Name
In mother's womb You are alone our Cherisher;
In this mortal world You are our only Sustainer (pause)."

(Sarang Mohalla 5, p-1215)

5- Namdev was a devotee of God and belonged to the low caste. He went into Hindu temple while singing the praises of the Lord. The high caste Brahmin priests threw him out of the temple because of his low caste. Hindu temples have only one door. Namdev went at the back of the temple and sat there singing the praises of his Lord. Namdev himself has written at two-three places that as he sang the praises, the Almighty God rotated the temple around and turned the door towards him and the back towards the priests. His Devotees are very near and dear to Him.

Some people say that we work for eight hours a day and bring checks. We make house payment, car payment and buy groceries, how God is the Cherisher? How is He bringing us up?

We have electricity in our homes. If we do not pay the electrical bill for six months, the electric workers will come and cut off the electric connection. It will be all dark. The Almighty God Who has given us so much light of the stars, the moon and the sun, do we ever pay any bill for that?

If there is no air, people would die out of suffocation. Is He a Cherisher or not?

If there is no water, there would be no produce. The whole world would die out of starvation. Is He not a Cherisher? A person asked a small child to bring a glass of water. When the child brought the water, he said, "Thank you very much." Why thanking a child?

The reply was that we were civilized people even if a small child had given you a glass of water, we must say, "Thank you". Very good civilization. The Almighty God Who has given us so much water, Have we ever thanked Him?

The Giver is giving us eternally. Even a mother forgets to feed the child. When she hears the child crying, she realizes that the child is hungry. But He never forgets to give. We the receivers, sometimes get weary of receiving but He never gets tired of giving:

"You the Supreme Provider, perpetually granting boons,
Thou art contained in my soul and life-breath.
All kinds of viands You grant for our consumption
Yet I, ungrateful, admit not a single of your benefactions."
(Basant Mohalla 5, p-1181 Guru Granth Sahib)

Guru Gobind Singh describes in his Swayias the bounties of the Almighty that He gives to all throughout the universe.

"To those who know Him He giveth;
To those who know Him not He also giveth;
He giveth to the earth; He giveth to the heavens;
O man, why waverest thou?
The beautiful and Holy Lord of wealth will care for thee."

Guru Gobind Singh describes God in his writing-Akal Ustat (Praise of the Immortal):

"May we have the protection of the Immortal Being[6]
May we have the protection of All-steel!
May we have the protection of All-death!
May we have the protection of Great-steel!

I bow to the One Primal God Who extended sea and land,
the nether regions, And the firmament.
He is the primal Being, unseen, and Immortal;
His light is manifest in the fourteen worlds.
He is contained in the ant as in the elephant;
He deemeth the rich and the poor alike;
He is unequalled, unseen, and eternal;
He is the Searcher of all hearts;
He is invisible, indestructible, and without distinguishing dress[7]
He is without passion, color, form, or outline;
He is devoid of caste marks of every kind;
He is the primal Being, peerless and changeless;
He hath no enemy, no friend, no father, no mother;
He is far from all and near all;
His dwelling is in sea and land, the nether and upper regions.

6- The tenth Guru invented new names for God - Akal (the Immortal), Sarbloh (All-steel), Mahanloh (Great-steel), Sarbkal (All-death), Mahankal (Great-death), Asidhuj, Asiketu, and Kharagketu (having the sword on His banner), Asipani (sword in His hand), that is, God as the impersonation and source of bravery.
7- Anbhekh. The word also means without form.

Boundless is His form, and boundless His voice;
In the shelter of His feet dwelleth Bhawani;[8]
Brahma and Vishnu have not found His limits;
The four-faced Brahma pointeth out that God is indescribable.
He made millions of Indras and Bawans[9];
He created and destroyed Brahmas and Shivas.
The fourteen worlds He made as a play;
And again blended them with Himself.
He made endless demons, deities, serpents, Celestials singers,
      Yakshas, Excellent and beautiful.
He is spoken of in the past, the future, and the present;
And He knoweth the secrets of every heart.
He is not attached to any one love;
He is contained in the light of all souls;
He recognizeth all people and all places;
He is free from death and immortal;
He is the invisible, imperceptible Being, distinct from all the world.
He is Immortal, undecaying, imperishable, and of changeless
      purpose.
He is the Destroyer and Creator of all;
He is the Remover of sickness, sorrow, and sin.
**He who with single heart meditateth on Him even for a moment
Shall not fall into Death's noose."**

8- Parbati or Durga- the consort of Shiva.
9- Indra is the god of rain and Bawan was the dwarf incarnation of Vishnu.

HOW WORLD WAS CREATED?

For millions and millions of years before the creation of the world, there was utter darkness and God Himself was sitting alone in Absolute Trance. There was no earth and no sky. There was no day and no night, no sun and no moon. There was no air and no water. There was no man and no woman, no caste and no birth and no death. There was no time. There was neither hell nor heaven. There existed no deeds and no religion, no Divine knowledge and no meditation. There was no contemplation, penance, no self-contentment, nor fasting nor worship. There existed no Vedas, Simirities nor Shastras (Hindu religious Texts) nor Kateib. There was no Brahma (according to Hinduism there is Trinity- Brahma is god who creates, Vishnu is god who cherishes. Finally there is Shiva, god who is responsible for death), no Vishnu and there was no Shiva.

His limit no one knows. It is through the Perfect Guru (God) that I have obtained this understanding, says Guru Nanak and describes this whole situation in Maru Mohalla 1, page 1035-36 of Guru Granth Sahib (Sikh Holy Scripture):

For countless ages, there was nothing but utter darkness;
There was neither earth nor sky ; only existed the Almighty
God's Infinite Will.
There was neither day nor night; neither sun nor moon but God
Himself alone sat in Absolute Trance. (1)

There existed neither sources of creation, nor of speech; neither air nor water;
There was neither creation nor destruction nor transmigration.
There were no continents, no underworlds, nor seven seas, nor rivers with the flowing of water. (2)

There was no heaven, no mortal world and no underworld;

Neither there was hell nor heaven; neither death nor time;
Hell and heaven, birth and death, there were none; there was
      no coming and going (in the world). (3)

There was no Brahma, Vishnu nor Shiva;
None else was seen but the One Absolute Lord.
Neither was there a female nor a male; neither caste nor birth;
      neither pleasure nor pain. (4)

There were then no celibates, no men of charity and no
forest-dwellers;
Neither were the adepts, nor seekers, nor dwellers in joy;
Neither the Yogis, nor the Jangams (wandering sages) nor the
religious garb and none called himself the supreme yogi
      (Nath). (5)

There was no contemplation, penance, self-control, fasting nor
worship.
Nor any who could speak of duality.
The Almighty Lord was in Absolute Bliss and valued Himself
      His Own Glory. (6)

There existed no ritual purity nor self-restraint nor Tulsi rosary
(Basil rosary).
There were no Krishna's milkmaids nor Krishna; neither cows
nor cowherd.
Neither magical rites nor superstitious frauds nor any player on
      flute (Krishna).(7)

There were no deeds, religion nor sweet fly of Maya (love of
materialism);
Eyes could see no distinction of caste and birth;
No noose of secular attachment nor was death writ on the

mortal's brow;
>nor did anyone meditate on anyone else. (8)

Neither existed then slander nor laudation; neither life nor body;
Neither the Gorakh (Guru of yogis) nor Machhindra
(his disciple);
Neither the Divine Knowledge nor meditation, nor the beginning of clans, nor
>was there the reckoning of the Accounts. (9)

There was no distinction of castes and creeds as between
Brahmins and Kashatriyas;
There existed neither deity nor temples nor holy cow nor
Gyatri Mantras(Hindu text);
There were no burnt offerings nor gratuitous feasts nor ablutions
>at sacred places nor worship (of the gods). (10)

There were neither the Mullahs nor the Qazis[1];
Neither the Sheikhas nor the Hajis (pilgrims to Mecca);
There was no subject, king nor worldly pride nor any assuming
>title of Glory. (11)

There was no love nor devotion; neither the mind nor the matter;
Neither friends nor companions nor origin from father and mother (drop & blood);
The Lord Himself was the Merchant and Himself the Trader,
such was His Will. (12)

Neither were then the Vedas, Semitic Texts, Simrities and
Shashtras;
Nor the reading of the Puranas (Hindu texts); neither the sunrise

---

1. Mullahs, Qazis, Sheikhs are the tittles of Muslim clergy.

nor the sunset;
He, the Lord, Himself was the Speaker and the Preacher
knowing only
    Himself His Unknowable Self. (13)

When such was His Will, He created the world and without
support sustained the firmament;
He created Brahma, Vishnu and Shiva and instilled in men the
    desire of attachment. (14)

Rare was the person whom the Guru caused to hear His Word;
He made His ordinance operative and watched over all.
He created continents, solar systems and the underworlds and
    from the Absolute Self He became Manifest. (15)

His Limit no one knows;
It is through the Perfect Guru(God)I have obtained understanding.
Says Nanak, "Wondrous are they who are imbued with Lord's
truth and by singing
    His Praises they are delighted." (16)

Guru Nanak further explains that before the Creation, the Infinite and
Boundless Lord sat in Absolute Trance for 36 Yugas or ages (Yuga, a
period of cosmic time, running into millions of years). There was utter
darkness all around and it happened as He Willed. The Guru describes it
in Maru Mohalla 1, page 1026 of Guru Granth Sahib:

"For numerous ages there was all-darkness;
And the Infinite and Boundless Lord was seated in Trance.
Alone and Detached Lord sat in inky darkness,
The world of strife was not yet born.   (1)

Thiswise passed the Thirty-six Yugas(ages),

And as was His Will so He, the Absolute Lord, Worked;
And there was no rival of His, He Himself being Infinite and
Boundless. (2) ...."

WHEN WAS IT CREATED?

What was the time, what moment, what was the lunar day, what
week day, what was the season and what was the month, when the world
was created? The Brahmins would have recorded in their scriptures, if
they had found the answer; nor the Qazis (Muslim priests) who scribe the
writing of Quran, know the answer. Neither the Yogis nor anyone else
know the lunar day, week day, season and the month when the world
came into existence. **The Almighty Creator who has created the world,
He Himself alone knows the time and none else.** Many try to describe God's discourse and each claiming to be wiser than the other. Great
is the Master, Great is His Name, whatever is there, proceeds only from
Him. Guru Nanak says if some one deems himself able to do, he shall not
look adorned on arrival in the court of the Almighty:

Pilgrimages, austerities, compassion, charity
All are approved if they bring even a grain of merit in God's eye.
Whoever heartily hears, believes and loves God's Name,
obtains salvation by thoroughly bathing in the shrine within
himself.
All virtues are Thine, O Lord, I have none.
Without cultivating virtuous qualities, Lord's devotional service
cannot be performed.
My obeisance is unto God, Who Himself is world wealth and
real Brahma etc.
and I utter His Praises.
God is True, Beautiful and all joys abide within His mind.
What was the time, the moment, the lunar day, the week day,
What was the season and the month, when the world was

Pearls of Sikhism

created?

Had the Puranas (Hindu Scriptures) referred to this, the Pandits
(Hindu priests) would have discovered the time.

Nor the Qazis (Muslim priests) who scribe the writings of
Quran, know the time.

Neither the Yogis nor anyone else knows the lunar day, week
day, season and month.

The Creator Who creates the world, alone knows the time.

How to express, how to praise, how to describe and to know
God?

Says Nanak! All give discourses about God and each one
thinks himself to be wiser than the other.

Great is the Master and great His Name and what He does
must happen.

Nanak! If some one thinks himself to be powerful to do things
or thinks himself to be knower of God, he will not be honored
in the next world.

(Pauri 21, Japji, page 4, Guru Granth Sahib)

Baba Farid (1173-1266) has been a very famous Muslim saint
and in his succession there lived Sheikh Brahm. Guru Nanak visited Sheikh
Brahm and religious discussion ensued. During the discussion it was pointed
out by the Sheikh that in one of Semitic religious scriptures it was written,
"In the beginning was the Word and the Word was with God, and the
Word was God." Guru Nanak explained that nothing was before God
and nothing is independent of God. The 'Word' that you are referring to is
also His creation.

Guru Nanak explained to Sheikh Braham that nothing was independent of God. All Creation including 'Word' is His Own making. He
further said that after the Absolute Trance, He then first created Hisownself
into Nam (Name- pronounced as Naam) when He made Himself manifest. He Assumed Name (Nam). Nam and God are not two different
entities but one and the same thing. Nam is His Ownself and at His Own

level. Then at the next level He created the Nature and Universe. Nam sustains all the universe and its inhabitants. A contractor constructs a building and after finishing the job, he leaves and some other person comes to occupy it. But the most important aspect of this universe creation is, the Guru explains that its Creator (God) has not left after creation rather He abides within it and feels delighted in dealing with it. Guru uttered the following Sabad :

"God, the Lord of Himself, First created Hisownself and Assumed He Himself Name;
He then created (secondary) Nature and Abiding within it, He beholds it with delight.
Thou art the Creator, the Beneficent One, in Thy Pleasure, Thou blessest all.
Thou art the Knower of all. Thou givest and takest life with a word.
Abiding within, Thou beholdest Thy Creation with delight."
                            (Asa Mohalla 1, Pauri 1, p-463)
God and Nam are one and the same. Nam sustains all universes and all beings:

"O Lord, Thy Nam sustains all beings;
Thy Nam is the support of all the worlds and universes.
By the might of Nam are sustained Simiritis, Vedas and Puranas.
By Nam's support the mortals hear Divine Knowledge and meditation.
Thy Nam is the support of the skies and underworlds.
Thy Nam is the support of all forms of life.
Thy Nam sustains all the worlds and spheres.
Men are saved by listening to Nam with their ears.
Whomsoever by His Grace He attaches to the devotion of Nam;

Saith Nanak, he gets liberation entering in the state of Bliss."
(Gauri Mohalla 5 (5-16 Asht.), p-284)

There was more discussion with Sheikh Brahm. At the end the Sheikh begged for Guru's blessings and requested," Sir, please bless the ship of my life reach heaven." Guru promised that his ship would reach heaven. Sheikh Brahm reiterated, "Not like this, please give me a firm promise." The Guru said, "Sheikh Brahm, your ship is already at the shores of heaven."

HOW WAS IT CREATED?

The scientists and researchers are trying hard to find the end of God's Expanse. Some talk about big bang theory while others talk about evolution. But the more they research, the more they are amazed with its vastness. In order to explore the solar system, a space probe hit its comet target on July 3, 2005 in a NASA directed mission that scientists hoped would reveal clues to how the solar system was formed. It marked the first time a spacecraft touched the surface of a comet, igniting a dazzling fireworks in the space. It was a milestone for the U.S. space agency, which hoped the experiment would answer basic questions about the origins of solar system.

Even if the scientists hit millions of comets, it would be hard for them to understand the mystery of the Infinite Lord. His regime is endless and limitless. No one can know God's limit. Humanity is as yet far far away from uncovering the mystery of His creation. Guru Nanak explains in Japuji (24), page 5 of Guru Granth Sahib:

".....Many yearn to know His bounds, but His limits are not found.

His Limit none can know.

The more we describe, the more yet is to be explored.

Great is the Lord and high His seat;

His Name is the highest over the high.

If anyone be as great high as He is, then alone he would know how high He is.

How great He is, only He Himself knows.
O Nanak! the compassionate Lord by His Grace bestows gifts."

The Divine Guru Nanak says about the Creation :
"Kita pasao eko kawao
Tis tey hoay lakh daryao."
(Guru Nanak- Japuji (16), p-3)

"One Word, and the whole Universe throbbed into being,
And lakhs of rivers began to flow."
(translation of the above)
The Divine Word explains that many times before also this
expanse was created
but in the end the One Absolute Lord remains always the Same:
"Kaee baar pasario pasaar
Sada sada ik Ekonkar."
(Gauri Sukhmani Mohalla 5, p-276)
"Many times this expanse was created,
Ever ever the Unique Lord God remains the Same."
(Translation of the above)
Now the Guru gives us a glimpse of God's Court or Darbar. He
describes it in Sarang Mohalla 5 Ashatpadi ghar 6 at page 1235-
36 of Guru Granth Sahib:

"Hear ye the Gospel of the Unknowable and Fathomless Lord;
Wondrous is the Court of the Transcendent God (Pause).

I am a sacrifice unto my Guru ever and forever more,
By the Guru's grace I sing the Infinite Praises of the Lord,
Lo, my mind is illumined from within
With the collyrium of wisdom, my ignorance is dispelled. (1)

Immeasurable is His Expanse.
His Glory is boundless and infinite.
Innumerable are His wondrous plays one can know not, nor
describe;
For, He is neither in Joy, nor in Sorrow. (2)

Millions of Brahmas utter His Praise through the vedas,
Millions of Shivas contemplate but Him alone;
With a particle of His Power, millions of persons become
His prophets.
Millions of Indras stand at the Door of the Lord. (3)

Myriads are winds, fire and waters;
Myriads are oceans of jewels, curd and milk.
Myriads are the suns, the moons and the stars;
Myriads are goddesses and gods of many kinds. (4)

Innumerable are the earths and Elysian Cows [2]
Innumerable are the wish-fulfilling trees and they whose lips
are on the flute (Krishnas);
Innumerable are the skies and nether regions;
Innumerable are supreme persons who dwell only on Him (5)

2- Elysian (Kamdhein) Cow and wish-fulfilling (Paarjaat) Tree : Hinduism narrates that the
gods churned the ocean and out of that came out 14 Jewels. Those 14 Jewels were:

1. Nectar, 2. Wine, 3. The Moon, 4. Elysian Cow,
5. Sublime Horse, 6. Elephant, 7. Poison, 8. Wealth,
9. Dhanatar Vaid (Physician), 10. Jewel, 11. Conch,
12. Elysian Tree, 13. Nymph, 14. The Bow.

It is believed that whatever you ask from 'Kamdhein Cow' and the 'Paarjaat
Tree', you will get it. Here the Hinduism is talking about only One Kamdhein Cow and One
Paarjaat Tree but the Guru is describing that there are innumerable Kamdhein Cows and
innumerable Paarjaat Trees in the Court of the Almighty.

There are millions of Shastras, Simiritis and Puranas(Hindu Texts),
And millions of men discourse upon Him in millions of ways.
Millions of listeners hear the praise of God, the Treasure of
Virtues,
For, He is in all life, He is the All-filling God. (6)

Innumerable are the Dharamrajas (celestial judges),
Innumerable gods of wealth;
Innumerable are the gods of water, Innumerable mountains of gold.
Innumerable are the Sheshnagas (thousand hooded serpents),
who utter His Ever-new Names;
They know not the limits of the Lord. (7)

Myriads are the universes and their parts;
Myriads are forms, colors and solar systems.
Myriads are forests, fruits and roots,
Yea, God is both Manifest and Unmanifest. (8)

Myriads are the Yugas (ages), days and nights.
Myriads are the world-destructions and myriads of creations.
Myriads are creatures in the Kingdom of His Home,
The Omnipresent Lord is filling all the places. (9)

Manifold is His Plays which one can describe not,
And manifold is His Power which He manifests in Innumerable
ways.
Myriads are the beauteous melodies which sing of the Lord,
Myriads of unmanifest scribes are seen there. (10)

He is the Highest of the high, with Whom abide His saints,
Throughout day and night, they sing His praises with love.
Millions of celestial strains sing of the Lord's supreme bliss,
Of that relish there is no limit and end. (11)

He is the True Lord and true is His Abode.
He is the Highest of the high, Immaculate and detached.
He alone knows the extent of His Own Doings,
And He pervades all hearts.
Nanak, the Merciful Master is the Treasure of Compassion,
And blessed are those, O Nanak, who contemplate Him. (12)

Guru Nanak traveled for 14 years to deliver Divine Message to the humanity. He went upto Tibet in the north and Ceylon in the south. He went as far out as Assam province (India) in the east and reached Baghdad (Iraq) in the west. He visited famous temples of the Hindus and also visited famous mosques of the Muslims. He went to the centers of the Sidhas and the Mathhs of the Yogis. He also visitedthe various saints and religious leaders and groups all over. He had religious discussions with the individuals as well as with groups small or large.

The objective of Guru Nanak's Guruship was to give instructions in the True Name, to save humanity from immersing in the ocean of distress and misery arising out of worldly life, and to blend the human souls with their Creator, thus, emancipating them from the cycle of transmigration breaking all barriers and bonds of sufferings. This is the fundamental character of Sikh Faith. Sikhism endeavors to uplift the human soul from the shackles of Maya (materialism). **It aims at a virtuous life which leads to the ultimate realization of a state of Eternal Bliss.**

Sikh chroniclers claim that the life of a recluse always got a honorable status in all the societies of India during the days of Guru Nanak. People who renounced life, were held in an elevated position and high esteem because the public believed that the hermit living in a forest had a pure life and he was closer to spiritual attainment. Yogis enjoyed influence over the common people and through display of their supernatural powers made people their followers. The expectation of their blessings and the fear of their curses created awe in people's mind and in terror they ministered their wants. Guru Nanak reached the Sumer-Parbat (also called Golden mountain) in Tibet where he met an assembly of 84 Sidhas. They asked him what power brought him there because ordinary man could not reach that place. The Guru replied that he repeated the Name of God and with loving devotion contemplated Him and that power brought him there. They inquired about the conditions prevailing in India. The Guru told them that falsehood overshadowed the land and the moon of truth was completely enshrouded in the darkness of ignorance. The kings were butchers and justice had taken wings and flown away. He further said, "Nathji, when the Sidhas are hiding themselves in mountain enclaves, who is left behind to lead the people in the right direction?" The Sidhas tried to create an impression of their miraculous and supernatural powers on him but failed. They thought that their creed was higher than Guru's creed and so they wanted to convert him to their own creed but could not succeed and ultimately they submitted before him. The Guru chastised them for removing themselves from the scene of human life where they could impart spiritual awakening among the human beings and take mankind across the ocean of suffering. On the contrary they lived in caves dug under the earth and came out only to answer the call of the nature. They blew something like a horn in the morning, in the evening and at night.

The Guru found serious lapses in the lives of Yogis-Sidhas. They retreated into the forests avoiding their moral and social responsibilities. There was so much evil and suffering in those days which the Yogis could remove by their spiritual knowledge. As they were the men of religion, they could purify the world of its impurities. It is recorded that Guru Nanak asked Bhangernath, the leader of the Yogis, during their discussion, "You become an ascetic separating yourself from the householders and then you go and beg at their doors for food." Thus the guru denounced them calling them as parasites on society. He disapproved the whole idea of retirement from worldly life and humbled the Yogis after his discussion with them and made them realize the futility of their doctrine. Upon this according to Bhai Gurdas (Var 1, pauri 44), the Yogis finally complimented the Guru and **said, "Hail, O Nanak, great are thy deeds! Thou hast arisen a great Being, and lit a Light in this age of Falsehood (Kalyug) in the world."** Guru attached importance to household life with all the responsibilities that go with it and thus put the Gristhi (family man) in an exalted state. A householder must face and assume all the moral and social duties even at the cost of all the suffering and not to be like the Yogis and Sidhas with their escapist attitude. In Sikhism all ascetic orders are decried. Sikh Gurus have given importance to putting restrain on human desires and lead a self-disciplined moral life. Human being must maintain indifference amidst the attractions of the world and should live desireless amidst the desires of the world. But the values required to sustain and preserve the life of a person as a natural human being are considered as survival needs and their attainment is regarded as necessary for achievement of higher qualities of life.

The Guru exhorts individuals to lead a life like a lotus untouched by the waves of water or the duck by the pond The hymns addressed to Yogis and Sidhas in Sikh Holy Scripture show that Guru Nanak wanted to cure them of their craze for miraculous powers. Instead they should have righteous deeds to redeem the society of its evils. The possession of miraculous powers is by itself not indicative of one's spiritual merit which comes from devotion to the Lord.

After visiting Mecca and Madina, Guru Nanak came to Baghdad. According to Muslim Shariat(Code of Law), music was forbidden there. The high ranking Muslim priests did not accept musical verses. Instead of condemning unethical, immoral and demoralizing poetry, they rejected music (Raga) completely. The whole of Sikh Holy Scripture is in devotional musical verses and in various forms of Ragas and Raganis. In the morning the Guru shouted the call for prayer in a musical tone, on which the whole population of the city was rapt in silent astonishment. He did it differently than the Muslims. Mardana played the rebec and the Guru started the Sabad Kirtan (musical recitation of Sikh Scripture - Gurbani). People were thrilled. The news spread in the whole city. The high priest, Pir Dastgir and many others came to see the Guru.

According to Mohammedans there are seven skies above the earth and seven nethers including the earth. The Guru recited the 22nd Pauri of Japuji, page 5 of Guru Granth Sahib:

"Counless the worlds beneath and countless the skies above,
No limit is found, nor Vedas have.
Eighteen thousand, say the Semitic Texts,
Vain is such count; Nothing is real but the One Essence.
His Infinity no one can measure or state,
Men's lives are finished counting but God's account finishes not.
He is Great, says Nanak,
He Himself knows His Oneself."

The Pir was wonder-struck hearing something contrary to the authority of the Holy Quran, that there were hundreds of thousands of nethers and upper regions. The Pir asked the Guru, "Do you think that Hazarat Mohammad was lying when he said there were seven nethers and seven skies while you say there are hundreds of thousands?"
The Guru replied, "No, he did not lie. He said what he saw. He only saw seven nethers and seven skies."
The Pir questioned Guru's word and asked him to give proof, to give manifestation of what he said.
The Guru said, "Ok, please come with me."
The Pir replied, " No, I cannot go because I am old, take my son."
The Guru asked Pir's son, "Come and close your eyes."

Bhai Gurdas-[3] explains in his Var-1 and Pauris 35-36 that Guru Nanak laid his hand on the Pir's son's head and showed him thousands and thousands of upper and lower regions as described above in the Pauri 22 of Japuji. To give proof whether the son actually saw the thousands of regions, he brought Parshad (sacred food) from one of those worlds and gave to his father when he opened his eyes. The Pir bowed before the Guru and asked for his blessings.

3- When the Sikh Holy Scripture (Guru Granth Sahib) was compiled first time,it was done by the fifth Sikh Guru, Guru Arjan Dev. The Guru gave the dictation and it was noted and written down by Bhai Gurdas. Bhai Gurdas compiled his own writings in Vars and Kabits and he is a recognized authority in Sikh theology.

When was the world created, no body knows and nobody can know except the Almighty Creator Himself. The Divine Word says:

"Ja Karta saristi kau sajai aapai janay soee."
(Japuji, page 4)
'The Creator Who created this world, alone knows the answer.'

(Translation of the above)

WHO GOES TO HEAVEN ?

There are many different religions in the world, some new and others very old. There are different religious Camps. Some of these camps believe in quantity. They are always in pursuit of increasing their memberships. In order to lure others to their creed, they give some guarantee for entry in the Heaven. Some of them not only offer the guaranteed entry in the Heaven but emphasize in such a way as if they are carrying the Keys to Heaven in their pockets. If one asks them, "What was happening to the world when your camp did not even come into existence? Was the whole world going to hell then? Or was there no world before that?" First came the Satyug (the Golden Age) the age of Truth. It had all the Four Feet[1] of Truth and the truth prevailed all around in this world. Then came Treta (the Silver Age) when one foot of Truth had gone. After that came Duaper (the Brass Age) which had only Two feet of Truth. Then arrived the Present Kalyug (the Dark Age). The Kalyug has only one foot of Truth to stand on. Falsehood , treachery and arrogance are the trade mark of Kalyug. If for a moment we accept their exclusive right of entry to heaven, where were the people going during these long ages? The claimants' camps came into existence only in the Dark Age which it is generally believed to have begun about five thousand years ago.

Who Goes to Heaven?

The followers of such camps are having the assurance of guaranteed entry into Heaven. National survey indicates that there is staggering

---

1- Any animal (chair or table) has four legs. Four feet (four legs) are considered to be the perfect situation. So Satyug (Golden Age) was the perfect age having four feet or legs of Dharma (truth) where nothing but truth prevailed all around. Some people say that the expected age was 100,000 years in that age. Then came Treta (Silver Age) where one foot of Dharma was lost and expected age of people was 10,000 years. In Duaper (Brass Age), two feet of Dharma (truth) had gone. The average age came down to 1,000 years. After that came Kalyug (Dark Age or the Wicked Age). Now is the Kalyug which is only standing on One foot of Dharma. The expected age is around one hundred years.

percentage of persons who commit adultery, both men and women cheating their spouses. People slander others and lie most of the time. Will Heaven accept adulterers, slanderers, liars or robbers also? If the answer is not in affirmative then who will go there? What would happen to their claim of guaranteed entry to heaven? If heaven can accept backbiters, adulterers, slanderers, cheaters or liars, who would go to hell then? If you ask anyone about going to heaven, one would be surprised to hear that majority are sure to reach heaven. Their answer would be, "My Lord will take me to heaven." Sure, your Lord can take you there but you will have to follow the instructions of your Lord first when he says, "Do not commit adultery, do not steel, robe or lie. Earn your livelihood by honest means and do praise and prayer of the Almighty regularly." The Divine Word says,

> "By obeying His Order, one is acceptable
> And shall then reach his Master's court."
>   (Asa di Var pauri (15) p-471, Guru Granth Sahib)

No Lord will stand by us if we remain indulged in these worldly vices.

Three Modes of Human Mind:

There are three modes or temperaments under which our minds remain occupied all the time.

I. Tamas or Tamo (Egotism): There are Five famous vices - Lust, Anger (wrath), Greed (avarice), Worldly Attachment and Ego. The whole world lives under their influence. When a person is fully occupied with these vices, he has a state of mind called Tamo (Tamas - Egotism).

II. Rajo (Rajas - Optimism): When a person has a zeal to move forward in life and has an act of progressive vision, he enters into Rajo mode. He still remains under the influence of these vices.

III. Sato (Satik - Pessimism): When a person goes towards spirituality, he enters into Sato mode. By meeting the society of the Holy, he has a desire to meet his Lord. He then tries to control the influence of the five vices and moves in the direction of saintlihood.

The whole world remains in the cycle of these three modes of the mind. As one sleeps and passes the night in dreams, the whole world passes its Night of Life in slumber full of delusions. But only those who take refuge in the teachings of their Guru (Lord), will remain awake during their Night of Life and would gain a fruitful end. The Divine Word says:

"The Simirtis and Shastras[2] discriminate between 'good' and 'evil',
    but know not the essence of the Real Thing.
Without the Guru, no one knows the Quintessence,
    know not the essence of the Reality.
The world is in Slumber, strayed by the Delusions of the Three modes,
    and thus the Night (of their life) passes.
By Guru's Grace, only those keep awake, in whose mind the Lord abides
    and who utter the Nectar-Word.
Says Nanak, 'He alone attains to the Quintessence (of Reality),'
    who is forever Attuned to the Lord, and passes his Night, Awake."
                    (Ramkali Moh. 3, Anand(27), p-920)

As long as the world remains in the cycle of Three Modes, there will be utter Delusions and Doubts. When the five vices are in full swing, they have overwhelming control over our minds. For fruitful life we must have control over these vices. When there is no salvation from the Three Modes, there will be no heaven and the cycle of death and rebirth will continue.

2 - Hindu Holy Scriptures.

"Living within the Three Modes, there is no Equipoise, for, thus,
     one wanders in Doubts.
What do reading, studying and talking avail a man if he misses
     the very Origin.
In the Fourth State (of Bliss) there is spiritual bliss and
Guruwards attain it."
                           (Sri Rag Moh. 3, p-68, Guru Granth Sahib)

What is the Fourth State:

In this world someone is white and someone is black or brown.
There is old, young or a child. There is a man and a woman. There is a
Christian, a Hindu, a Muslim or a Jew. We distinguish all kinds of objects
around us. But when we climb a 50-storey building and then see down-
wards towards the same crowd, we cannot distinguish, who is white and
who is black; who is man and who is woman; who is young and who is
old; who is Christian and who is Muslim? All look alike from the top of the
building.

In the same way human beings make all kinds of distinctions un-
der the influence of Three Modes. But if by the Grace of the True Guru, he
climbs the 50-storey building of spirituality, **he comes in touch with the
Reality, vista of mind is opened and one has the Glimpse of the
Divine. Then everything looks the same to him. He sees the same
Divine Light equally shining in everybody. The Divine Word says:**

"Amongst all there is Light. That light art Thou
By His Light, the light shines equally within all the souls."
                                          (Dhanasri Moh. 1, p-663)
All the walls of the so called religions are broken, there is no religion.
There is One God, One Supreme Being and Only One Religion where
everything is equal:
"Amongst all the religions, the most sublime is the Religion of

God;
Of all the rituals and deeds, the work of God's service is the
most sublime."

(Basant Mohalla 5, p-1182)
The man sees the same Sublime Power in every direction where every-
thing is under His Command. There is no high and no low but it is all His
Play. Divine Word (Guru Granth Sahib) says:
"First, God created His Light and then by His Omnipotence
made all mortals.
From the One Light has welled up the entire universe. Then
who is good or who is bad?
O men, stray ye not in doubt.
For the Creator is in the Creation and the Creation is in the
Creator.
He is fully filling all places. (Pause)
The clay is the same but the Fashioner has fashioned it in
myriad ways.
There is no fault with the vessel of clay, nor there is any fault
with the potter.
The One True God is midst all and it is He alone Who
creates all.
Whosoever realizes His Will, knows the One alone, yea, he
alone is the servant of God.
The Unknowable Lord is seen not. The Guru has
blessed me with sweet molasses.
Says Kabir: my doubt is dispelled and now I have seen the
Immaculate God in all."

(Prabhati, Kabir, p-1349-50)

SEHAJ (Fourth State of Mind):

A key-term, representing the process of realization and spiritual
ascent, is **Sehaj.** Sehaj is state of Turiya, above the Three Modes (quali-

ties). It is transcendental state, it stands for enlightenment, serenity, spontaneous devotion. The path of Sehaj lies in the realization of the self through the process of prayer, meditation and devotion. It is a path of devotion that involves no 'forced' process of self-purification. It does away with all rituals, fasts, observation of 'sacred' days and hours and caste-rituals, the path of Hatha yoga (yoga of forced effort), observation of codes like the yogi's wearing of earrings, blowing of the horns, carrying a patched coat and smearing the body with ashes etc.

and also occult practices. All rites and rituals are done away with. The true Guru's disciple, practitioner of Sehaj, need not retire to the forest or mountain cave but engaging in prayer in the early morning hours through reciting Gurbani (Divine Word) and also performing or listening to Holy music (Kirtan) lauding the Creator and leading the life of a true householder according to the code of conduct laid down by the Guru through the Divine Word.

In essence the path of Sehaj (Fourth State of Mind) lies in exploring spirituality and the apprehension of the Divine Presence in all Creation. A devotee reaches a state of mind where celestial joy and bliss (Sehaj-Anand) will descend upon him. His life becomes Nature oriented, whatever happens, he lauds the Creator in return with thankfulness and submits to the Almighty.

The Ashatvadi 6 of Sri Rag, Mohalla 3, page 68 of Guru Granth Sahib has fully illuminated different facets of Sehaj:

> "The whole world seeks to attain the state of Equipoise (Sehaj)
>   but without the Guru (Lord), it is not attained.
> Exhausted with learning, Pundits[3] and Astrologers
>   Fall in sects and into delusion, are lost.
> The state of Poise is attained only on meeting the Guru
>   Should the Lord in His Will show Mercy.   (1)
>
> O brother! There is no Poise (Sehaj) without the Guru.

3- Learned Hindu Brahmins.

It is from the Divine Word (Sabad) that poise proceeds and
that True God is obtained. (Pause)

Divine laudation with spontaneous devotion becomes acceptable
without it is all useless utterance.
Thus is all Worship that devotion emanates and thus is all Love
and Detachment.
In the state of Poise is utter Bliss and Peace,
Without it life is all a waste.   (2)

Spontaneously then Praise thy Lord and enter into the Silence
of Great Peace[4].
Utter His Virtues and in deep devotion get absorbed.
Through the Word God dwells in the mind and tongue tastes
God's Nectar.   (3)

By entering the Sanctuary of the True One, death is easily
destroyed[5]
If a person practices the true way of life, God's Name abides
in his mind.
Exceedingly fortunate are they who have found God and easily
remain absorbed in Him.   (4)

There is no Equipoise in Maya (worldly wealth). Maya abides
in Duality.
The egoist's actions brings torments of egoism.
Of such transmigration is not ended.
And ever are they born and die.   (5)

---

4 - Sehaj Samadh: In contradistinction to the Yogi's trance, which he brings about through
Hatha Yoga, the Sikh enters into the trance spontaneously by concentrating his mind on the
Word (Sabad).
5- There is no fear of death.

Living within the Three Modes, there is no Equipoise,
    for, thus, one wonders in Doubt.
What do reading, studying and talking avail a man if he misses
the very Origin.
In the Fourth State (of bliss) there is Spiritual Bliss and the
        Guruwards (who belongs to Guru) attain it.   (6)

The Name of God, the Unmanifest, is the true treasure-
The realization thereof comes in the serene Transcendent State.
The Virtuous praise God saying, ' True is the reputation of the
True One'.
The Lord unites even the strayers. It is through the Name
(Word) that union is accomplished.   (7)

Without attaining the transcendent state all is blind
    And storms of Maya - Delusion.
Through this State comes realization,
      By means of the Immeasurable Holy Word (Sabad).
And the Guru-God, in His Mercy, unites man with Himself. (8)

Through Equipoise,the Unseen,Fearless,Luminous and Formless
    Lord is recognized.
Of all the beings, there is but One Bestower. The Luminous
    Lord is the blender of man's light with Himself.
Praise then through the Perfect Word (Gurbani)[6] thy Lord,
    Who is beyond end and beyond limit.   (9)

The Wise-in-God have the Name as their wealth and through
    Equipoise do they Trade (with Him).
Night and day, they reap the Profit of the Lord's Name
    Whose Treasures are Inexhaustible?
Nanak: When the Giver gives, he never falls

---

6 - Divine Word uttered by the Sikh Gurus - contents of Guru Granth Sahib.

Short (of the Gifts). (10)

Those who are in Fourth State are almost in the Heaven. As long as one Remains in the cycle of Three Modes, one cannot enter heaven. Bhagat Ravidas enumerates his experience of the heaven. He calls that place a city by the name of Begampura meaning that there is no fear, no worry and no grief. There is no pain and no care. There are no taxes on the goods. Such is the wonder of my Fatherland that there is always Peace and Calm. There is One Lord who rules over there. There is no second or third but all are alike and equal. There abides only the Rich (with Nam) and Content and they can go anywhere they want, there is no restriction. They know the Mansion of their Lord and nobody prevents them to go there.

Whosoever is the citizen of that city, is my friend, says Ravidas:

"Begampura is the name of the city.
At that place there is no pain or care.
There is no fear of tax on goods there.
Neither awe, nor error, nor dread or decline there.
I have now found an excellent abode.
My brethren, there is ever-lasting safety there. (Pause)
Firm, stable and for aye is the sovereignty of God.
There is no second or third, He alone is there.
Populated and ever famous is that city.
The wealthy and content dwell there.
As they please, so do they stroll about.
They know the Master's Mansion, so none does obstruct them.
Says Ravidas, the emancipated shoe-maker, he, who is his
Fellow-citizen, is also his friend."
(Rag Gauri Ravidasji p-345, Guru Granth Sahib)

What is Bliss! It is a wonderful experience of absorption in the Absolute wherein all desires are annulled. It can be felt by meditating on His excellences and rejoicing in His Name. It is a state of mind when a devotee is intensely attached to the beloved Lord and is fully resigned to His Supreme Will. It is the devotion of a person when the body and the soul both are dedicated to Him. It is a stage of complete submission and endless patience to give in to His Will. Even the most unfavorable circumstances of life are regarded as His Sweet Will. Such a person is not subject to transmigration but is immersed in God which is a perfect communion with the Divine. The attainment of this heavenly Bliss is the goal of Sikh endeavor. This celestial bliss can neither be heard with ears nor uttered by the tongue. Pen cannot write it and language cannot describe it. It is the achievement of emancipation from Maya (materialism) and finally union with the Lord which is the highest state of spiritual Glory. Bhagat (saint) Kabir in one of his devotional hymns had asked for this Superb Ecstasy (Jiwan Mukti) and liberation from all ills during his life time. He showed complete disinterestedness in heaven. According to his expression in the hymn neither the admission into heaven nor the mere release from the cycle of rebirth and death is as high a goal as communion with God. To reach this stage only love of God should dominate every other love which is the ultimate end of all religious and spiritual quests. This is the highest ideal which Guru Nanak set before humanity. How is it realized? Guru explains:

"All talk of bliss but the Real bliss is realized only through the Guru,
When one knows eternal bliss from the Guru, then the Loved Lord shows His mercy unto him.
In His mercy the Lord dispels our evil and blesses us with the collyrium of enlightenment.
They, who have become detached within, their Word of the True Lord embellishes.
Says Nanak: Such indeed is the bliss which one knows from the Guru."

(Ramkali Moh. 3, p-917)

SIKHISM AND HEAVEN:

Sikhism does not believe to convert others to its fold. Sikhs never tell others to join Sikh Religion. Guru Nanak never said to people that they would go to heaven only if they had become his disciples. Sikhism never preaches, never believes and never claims that only Sikhs can go to heaven and none else. When sun shines, it shines all over the world. So **Guru Nanak (the Divine Guru) stood guarantee to the entire Humanity saying that whosoever one may be irrespective of caste, creed, race, sex, color, religion or nationality:**

"He shall become pure whosoever repeateth His (God) Name With devotion, affection and heartfelt love."
(Gauri Sukhmani Moh. 5, p-290)

'He shall become pure' means that with praise and prayer of the Almighty he will come out of the grip of the Five Vices and then shall move towards his goal of heaven. Divine Word says:

"Prayer and Praise of the Almighty removeth the impurities of mind
And the Ambrosial Nam then filleth the mind."
(Gauri Sukhmani Moh. 5, p-263)

By Glorifying the Divine through the Nectar-Word, one gains the Divine qualities or values in the process. Suppose a robber robs 10 banks every day. When he starts sincerely and honestly the praise and prayer of the Almighty, the negative influence of these vices will start loosen up and one day soon he will rob 9 banks instead of 10. Then 8, 7, 6........... and one day he will not rob any bank. And then through the process of praise and prayer, he will start moving towards positive direction and ultimately towards saintlihood. **Mere talk of so called heaven will not take us anywhere. The Divine Word says:**

"By mere talk man goes not to Heaven
The Deliverance is by the practice of Truth alone."
(Slok Moh. 1, p-141)

Sikhs are not afraid of hell nor they are desirous of the so called Heaven. There is something beyond heaven too and that is God Himself. If a bucket of water is thrown in the ocean, the water of the bucket also assumes the appearance of the ocean itself. The Praise and Prayer of the Almighty God, shall give rise to Nam (Name of God) inside the mind and a person is reborn in the spirit of the Guru. As water blends with water, our souls blend with the Supreme Soul and then there is no Heaven nor Hell but Eternal Bliss. There is no more separation from the Divine, there is no more coming and going into the world. The Divine Word says:

> "His soul and body dyed with the Name of One God
> Shall ever abide with the Supreme Soul.
> As water blendeth with water,
> So light is blended with Divine Light.
> Transmigration is ended and rest obtained-
> Nanak is ever a sacrifice to the Lord."
>   (Gauri Sukhmani Moh. 5, p-278)

The essential character of Sikh Faith is that it endeavors to uplift the human soul from the shackles of materialism. It aims at a virtuous life and attainment of the highest pinnacle of spiritual advancement which leads to the realization of Supreme Bliss. Spiritual development is the ultimate goal of Guru's Sikh. Therefore, a Sikh does not aspire for an empire or strive for salvation but the ultimate goal of a Sikh is to become one with Unmanifest One and to merge with the Almighty Lord.

> "I desire not empire and I desire not salvation (heaven)
> I crave for nothing but the love of Thy Lotus-Feet."
>   (Dev Gandhari Moh. 5, p-534)

A Sikh is only desirous for the Holy Sight of the Lord and cares not for heaven or deliverance:

> "He who drinks in the Guru's teaching through the Nectar-
> Word is Approved.

He seeks the Sight of the Lord at His Gate
Of what account to him, then, heaven or Deliverance?"
(Asa Moh. 1, p-360, Guru Granth Sahib)

"What is hell and what poor heaven?
God's saints reject both of them.
Through the Grace of my Guru, I owe not any obligation to either."
(Ramkali Kabir, p-969)

"As long as the mind cherishes hope for the heaven
So long does one abide not at the Lotus-Feet
I know not if Paradise has a moat and ramparts or is plastered
with mud
Nor know I of the gate of Paradise
Saith Kabir: what else can I say now,
Except that the Holy Congregation alone is the Real Heaven."
(Bhairon Kabir, p-1161)

CONCEPT OF NAM (DIVINE NAME)

According to Gurmat (Guru's teaching) before the creation, God lived absolutely by Himself, Formless. When He made Himself manifest, He first formed Himself into Nam (pronounced as Naam) and then created Nature. After creating Nature, He did not go away from it, rather He sustained His creation with His Own presence into it and felt delighted.

> "God Himself created His ownself and assumed Himself the Name
> Secondly He then created Nature and seated within it, He
> beholds it with Delight.
> Thou Thyself art the Donor and Creator,
> Being pleased Thou bestoweth and showest mercy.
> Thou art Knower of all, Thou givest and takest life with a word.
> Abiding within, Thou beholdest Thy creation with delight."
> (Asa Mohalla 1- pauri 1, p-463 Guru Granth Sahib)

A): Nam (Divine Name) and God are not two different entities. Nam is just another aspect of the Almighty, still Formless. Nam is the total expression of all that God is. Nam sustains everything:

> "Nam sustains and controls all beings,
> Nam supports the universe and its regions.
> Nam sustains the Simiritis, Vedas and Puranas,
> Nam sustains the processes of listening, enlightenment and meditation.
> Nam is the prop of the skies and under-worlds.
> By the might of Nam are sustained all beings.
> Nam is the support of all the worlds and spheres.
> All by listening to the Holy Nam find liberation.
> He, whom He mercifully attaches to His Name,
> O Nanak, obtains salvation and gets into the fourth state of beatitude."
> (Gauri Sukhmani Mohalla 5, 16-5, p-284)

B): Nam is not expressed as mere noun and it does not mean that there is a special name of God and by enchanting of which, one will meet Him. God is Infinite and can be called by infinite names, but who can count His Infinite Names? The enlightened and the blessed ones remember Him through His Attributes:

> "God hath no marks, no color, no caste, no lineage,
> No form, no complexion, no outline, no costume; none can in
>   any way describe Him.
> He is Immovable, Fearless, Luminous, and measureless in might;
> He is accounted King of kings, Lord of millions of Indras;
> He is Sovereign of the three worlds, demigods, men, demons;
>   The woods and dales declare Him Indescribable.
> **O Lord, who can tell all Thy Names? The wise call Thee special
> names according to Thy deeds."**
>
>   (Guru Gobind Singh- Jap Sahib)

C): God may be called by countless names by the devotees who create these name according to His Attributes and qualities, but the first and the foremost name of God is clearly depicted as 'SAT' (Eternal Truth) which shows the ever existence of God:

> "Our tongue utters only Thine acquired Name
> But 'SAT NAM' (Eternal Truth) is Thy Primal and
> Transcendental Name."
>
>   (Maru Mohalla 5, p-1083 Guru Granth Sahib)

D): The word NAM (Name) is used in practical religious life and in discipline of meditation. God is remembered by His Attributive Names. In Sikhism "Waahay-Guru" is the True Name to be meditated upon which represents the total power of God. Other religions have given the Divine Names like Ram, Allah, God etc. Contemplation or meditation on True Name (WaahayGuru) is called practicing the presence of God in our consciousness.

E): Gurbani (Divine Word) itself is NAM: Gurbani is the Divine Word which came through Guru Nanak (from the mouth of the Guru) and his successor Gurus direct from God. That Divine Word is the Sikh Holy Scripture (Guru Granth Sahib).

I)- Gurbani is Nam:

> "The Guru's Word is the (Lord's) Name:
> > This Name I enshrine in my heart.
> Dwelling on the True Guru, the mind bird comes under one's sway;
> Saith Nanak: If He, the Lord, becomes merciful,
> > One is Attuned to the Name."
> > > (Sarang ki Var, pauri, p-1239)

ii)- The term 'Nam Japo' (or Nam Japna) means to remember God and to invoke His   Presence in our consciousness. All modes of meditation take the devotee into the presence of God, but Hari Kirtan (musical recitation) of Gurbani, is the Super form of meditation. It invokes one's consciousness to the maximum level, into the Presence of God:

> "Glorious is the Lord's praise and the Lord's Name,
> It is the Sublimest Deed in the Dark Age."
> > (Kanre ki Var Mohalla 4, p-1314)

iii)- Salvation cannot be attained without Nam. In other words, anything that delivers salvation is Nam. Since Gurbani delivers salvation, therefore, Gurbani is Nam:

> "The True Bani is the sweet-nectar
> Whosoever is devoted to it, attaineth salvation."
> > (Malar Mohalla 1, p-1275)
> "Whosoever devoted to Eternal Bani
> Will get deliverance."
> > (Dhanasri Mohalla 1, p-661)

"Whosoever lauds the Ambrosial Gurbani
One obtains the Immortalizing Name Nectar."
(Majh Mohalla 3, p-118)
It is, therefore, very clear that any form of recitation of Gurbani, simple reading with attention and devotion, or meditation on any Sabad (Word) of Gurbani or Kirtan (musical recitation) of **Gurbani is fully deemed as Nam Japna (mediation on Nam),** that is to invoke the presence of God in one's consciousness.

iv)- Gurbani is Guru:

"Gurbani is the embodiment of the Guru and Guru is the em bodiment of Gurbani
In Gurbani are contained all the Nectars,
If the devotee accepts what the Word Proclaims, the Guru in person saves him."
(Nat Mohalla 4, p-982)

Gurbani is Nirankar(Formless):

"Wauh, Wauh (wonderful) Bani is the Formless Lord.
There is none so Great as He."
(Slok Mohalla 3, p-515)

Gurbani is all Nad, Ved:

"The Guru's Word (Gurbani) is the Nada[1], the Guru's Word is the Veda;
For, through it, one is Imbued with the Lord of the Universe,
In it is contained the merits of all austerities, fasting and pilgrimages."
(Ram kali Mohalla 1, p-879)
It is, therefore, Nam that ultimately leads a person to Eternal Bliss. For God consciousness, one must come in contact with Nam, but with-

1- In the Yoga Philosophy, the nasal sound represented by a Semi-circle.

out Guru one cannot attain Nam and would wander away in the darkness:
> "Were a hundred moons to appear
> Were a thousand suns to arise
> There would still be utter darkness
> If there were no Guru."

(Asa di Var, Mohalla 2, p-463)

> "Let no one in the world remain in doubt
> That it could ever be possible to be saved without the Guru."

(Gaund Mohalla 5, p-864)

> "In this age of falsehood, Nam lieth hidden
> Though the Lord filleth all hearts,
> The Jewel of Nam becomes manifest in the hearts of only those
> Who resort to the Guru's refuge."

(Parbhati Mohalla 3, p-1334)

> "All repeat God's Name, yet He is not attained
> But when through the Grace of the Guru
> God comes to reside in the mind
> It is only then one's life becomes fruitful."

(Gujri Mohalla 3, p-491)

Nam and Human Being: According to all eastern religions, there are 8.4 million lives in the world. Half of them are in the water while other half are on the land and in air.

> "For several births thou wert a worm and a moth;
> For several births an elephant, a fish, a deer;
> For several births a bird, a serpent;
> For several births yoked as a bull, a horse;
> Meet thou the Lord of the Universe (God), for, now is the time,
> After ages thou has attained to the glory of human birth,
> (pause)."

(Gauri Guareyre Mohalla 5, p-176)

After going through lower species we got human life. It is, therefore, very precious. Human being is supreme in a hierarchical chain of His creation.

Emancipation of the soul is possible only through human form. Only man has the opportunity and capacity for the spiritual and moral progress. No religion and no philosophy can exist without human being. When the Gurus and the saints sing the Glory of the Lord, they sing it to human being because he has the awareness of the Divine. Guru Nanak makes him aware of his origin:

> "O my mind, thou art the spark of the Divine Light,
> So realize thy origin."
> (Asa Moh. 3, Chhant Ghar 3, p-441)

Sikh Gurus praise the nobility of man since he alone has the capabilities of achieving the Divine qualities. The exhortation - "Nam Japo", by the Gurus is directed towards man exclusively because the highest spiritual goal is within the reach of human being only. (Concept of 'Nam Japo' aims at spiritual evolution and development of human soul). Such are the great qualities of this humanly creature. Shakespeare in one of his works, "Hamlet" saluted him by calling him "a marvelous piece of work" created by God. Given such a high status and with his supremacy over everything else, he does not have the power to pull himself up by his own bootstraps and cross through peril and suffering of material life. Nor can he achieve salvation of his own soul without the help of some supernatural power. In Sikh Holy Scripture this supernatural power is defined as "Nam (Name of God)". Nam is the sole refuge for a man tossed about in the furious ocean of worldly existence. The essential trait of Sikh Religion is Nam (Naam). It is the central theme in the hymns of Guru Granth Sahib. Power of Nam is glorified and admired in Sikh Scripture. It is Nam that sustains all beings and the whole universe. Nothing is so perfect that it could or would exist apart from and independent of Nam (Him). The objective of Guru Nanak's Guruship was to give instructions in the True Name and to save humanity from immersing in the ocean of distress and misery arising out of the worldly life, and to blend the human souls with their Creator. There is only one thing in Sikhism, it is the Nam in the house of Guru Nanak:

"The Lord has given Nanak the gift of this game
That in his house resounds only the Name."

(Bhairon Moh. 5, p-1136)

WHY MEDITATION (Nam Japna) IS NECESSARY?

Under the materialistic comfort and progress, we forget God and never feel the urge of Nam Japna. But the Divine Word explains that without Nam the whole life has no value. Why is it so necessary to remember God? **Religion is not science, it is a Faith. If one has firm Faith then it is gold.**

1.   Whatever power is working inside our body and sustaining it when it leaves us the body is dead. It is then cremated or buried. As body is dead without life so life itself is dead without Nam. Without Nam our soul will wither away.

2.   When a person is dead, where does the soul go? The soul does not die. It takes some other form human or animal according to the Divine Ordinance which judges our daily activities in this life. Before it takes that form after leaving the body, it goes to God's court for final judgment. That journey for the soul is long and tedious. It comes across numerous hurdles on the way. For example when we travel from Los Angeles to New York, we take our car and enter the freeway. After some hours of drive the car runs out of gas and we also need something to eat. We take the exit, fill up the tank with gas, get something to eat and then hit the road again. Suppose we have no money, no credit card and we do not know anybody on the way. That will be horrible predicament with no help insight. Sikh Divine Word explains that the soul has long journey ahead of it. During our life time we work hard and save some money so that we spend our old age in comfort and peace. Similarly when we remember God (Nam-Japna - meditation) and utter His Name in all awareness, we accumulate wealth

of Nam and in return build credit in our account for the benefit of our soul. Hearing Lord's Name, repeating and chanting His praises with our tongue throughout the span of life, helps our soul at the time of need. The road that leads to God's court has countless miles and Lord's Name will be its food and companion. When the soul wanders in pitch darkness during its journey, the Light of God's Name will show the path. When it has no company, He shall guard it. Nam will cover the soul with shade where there is heat. When it is thirsty, God shall rain with nectar and quench its thirst. When it is in deep distress only His mercy can save it from those agonizing moments. Nam is the ladder to climb to salvation, the raft for crossing the ocean of transmigration thus liberating the soul from worldly torment helping it rest in peace and not being chastised by Yamas (couriers of death). **A body is dead without life and life itself is dead without Nam.**

Sikh Scripture repeatedly urges its disciples to dwell on His Glory to attain celestial tranquility. Singing His excellences brings everlasting solace to inner self of human beings. Taking refuge in Him emancipates the soul from all material bondages. His mercy saves our honor by forgiving all our sins and writing off our omissions and commissions. **The forgiving power of the Merciful God can nullify the law of retribution, the dictum- "As you sow so shall you reap."** It is the innate nature of our Master that He leaves us not when we seek His protection. This is the teaching of our immaculate Guru Nanak, the king of kings. **Sikhs should remember that the message of their great Master does not get diluted nor polluted amidst the forces of modernism and industrialization and the torch of His spiritual light is not extinguished.** Before Guru Nanak arrived in this world, minds of the masses had been enclosed in the rigid framework of rituals and ceremonial acts. Groups of factions based on different sets of dogmas and creeds had emerged. Yogis and recluses were preaching and practicing husk, the outer shell and not the spirit of religion. Guru Nanak sought to purge the society of its superstitions and meaningless rituals. Spiritual stature is judged not from the external mode of behavior but from the sincerity and earnestness of the inner self. With great poetic power he preached his lofty ideals and exhorted people not to let go the moral and spiritual anchor. Guru Nanak's religion brings out the best and the noblest in human beings. He awakened the souls of the people and guided them towards the right and spiritual path. **He who worships the Immaculate, shall become immaculate. He who worships the changing or the decaying, will himself change or decay.**

If we do not have any wealth of Nam in our account, imagine what will happen to us on the way to God's court after death?

"The journey whose distance is immeasurable
There, the Name of the Lord is thy food.
The journey upon which one goes in utter darkness
There, the Lord's Name is one's Light.
On the way where there is no acquaintance of thine
There, God's Name is thy recognition.
Where in utter Wilderness there is Heat and Fire
There, the Lord's Name is thy (only) Shade.
Where thirst tears thy mind
There, O Nanak, the Lord's Nectar rains on thee."
(Gauri Sukhmani Mohalla 5, 2(4), p-264)

3.   Upon death, couriers of death come and drag a person by hair. One will be powerless. Only Nam will save from the wrath of the couriers of death.

"When Death's myrmidon comes and seizes thee by the hair and knocks thee down
        On that day thou shalt be powerless.
Thou rememberest and contemplatest not God, nor practiced Compassion,
        You will be struck in the Face.
When the Righteous Judge asks for thy account, what face shalt

thou show him?

Saith Kabir: Listen O devotees of God!

In Holy company shalt thou find liberation."

(Kabir Maru, p-1106 Guru Granth Sahib)

4.   The cycle of death and rebirth will continue unless it is broken. **There is one and only one way to break it, is NAM. It is only the Name of God (NAM) that can break it:**

One cannot buy happiness and one cannot buy health either. These are the gifts of Nam in life. **This is why Meditation (Nam Japna) is necessary if we want to achieve happiness in this life and Salvation of the soul hereafter.**

"By great good fortune is obtained the gift of human body,
They who remember not God's Name are self-murderers.
Those forgetful of the Lord, of shame should die,
Without the Name of what avail is the life?
Eating, drinking, playing, laughing and making ostentations,
Of what use are the decorations of the dead?
They who hear not the Praise of the Supreme Bliss,
Are worse than the beasts, birds and species of creeping creatures.
Says Nanak, the Guru has implanted God's Name within me,
The Lord's Name alone abides within my heart."

(Gauri Mohalla 5, p-188)

SALVATAION - THE WAY TO GOD:

Sikh faith rejects all the claims of Yoga, mortification of body, self-torture and penances or retirement from life. **Gurus forbid the worship of anything of the Creation as a means to attain salvation of the soul. In Sikh monotheistic concept an Absolute and Only One God, the Formless and the Creator of the world is to be Glorified.** Devotion should be offered only to the Absolute One and not to His incarnations. His supremacy should be asserted over everything else.

Sikh faith aims towards the elevation of human soul to the heights of attunement with the Lord and paying homage to His Divine attributes. There is no place for formal ritualism. Without complete loyalty to the Guru, Sikh faith would be buried deep under a heap of senseless dogmas, meaningless rituals and ceremonial acts. Guru's word should be supreme in our daily existence without which life will be impure and polluted and will be in a deplorable condition which will lead to spiritual degeneration.

The road that leads us to God is the most difficult and complex one. But Guru Nanak has made this road simple and crystal clear by showing us a technical approach. He explains that life before it obtained human form, has been through different lower species. It has gathered along the way the impurities of every life it has passed through. Human mind has, thus, become quite black with these impurities:

"The impurity of many births hath attached to man's mind
And it has become quite black."
(Slok Mohalla 3, p-651)

As long as the human mind remains impure, it will not merge with the One Who is Absolute and Pure. How does the mind become pure?

"Nanak is Thy trader; Lord! Thou art my capital,
Then alone, the doubts depart from the mind, when I praise and pray to Thee."
(Rag Wadhans Mohalla 1, 557)

Those who have done it, have crossed the ocean of Maya (materialism) and merged with Him:

"Thou art the True Lord, Beautiful is Thy Praise
He who utters it, is saved."
(Slok Mohalla 1, p-469)

EXPLANATION: If a glass is full of dirty water, pour pure water into it constantly. The constant pouring of pure water into the glass will throw the dirty water out and ultimately the glass itself will be full of pure water.

In the same way the constant prayer and praise of God, will clean the impure mind. Human mind is in a chaotic state. It is full of five vices - lust, anger, greed, attachment and pride or ego. These are the obstacles in the Realization of Nam. Purity of mind is needed for spiritual uplift. No man nor monk can achieve salvation without disciplining the world of inner chaos. This discipline of inner chaos by banishing these five vices from the mind, is a prerequisite for spiritual excellence which is commanded by the Sikh Gurus. Singing the Glory of the Lord, the Mighty King, will help purge the mind of its impurities. By glorifying the Divine, the human mind imbibes divine qualities during the process. As a result when all the impurities are gone, Nam will enshrine the pure mind. This will lead to exalted mental state from the chaotic state. Spiritual evolution and development of mind will occur resulting in Heavenly Bliss. It is a profound awakening of the human soul:

"Prayer and Praise of God, shall give rise to Nam inside."
(Ramkali Mohalla 3-Anand, p-917)

Gurmat (Guru's teaching) further states that when hands are smeared with ordinary dirt, simple water will wash it away. If urine makes the cloth dirty, ordinary water cannot wash it, only soap will clean it. Similarly when our mind is full of impurities (sins), it needs some strong detergent and that detergent is Nam:

"As hands or feet besmirched with slime,
Water washes white; As garments dark with grime,
Rinse with soap are made light; So when sin foils the soul,
Prayer alone shall make it whole."
(Japji- pauri 20, p-4 Guru Granth Sahib)

That is the stage a true devotee yearns for. By prayer and praise of the Lord, one's mind comes in touch with Nam and becomes illuminated. Nam is registered by the consciousness and penetrates into the human soul and mind. As a result enlightened mind emerges and a person is reborn in the spirit of the Guru, he begins to make spiritual progress slowly. This glorious transformation or metamorphosis helps transcend human soul to a state of Absolute Bliss. It is a change in a person which occurs within the self from one form to another. The aspect of realization of God changes within and lifts the devotee from the Personal to Impersonal. All boundaries, limitations and barriers are broken and the individual soul starts merging with the Supreme Soul, as water blends with water, the light of human soul blends with Divine Light:

"His soul and body dyed with the Name of One God
Shall ever abide with the Supreme Soul.
As water blendeth with water,
So light is blended with Light.
Transmigration is ended and rest obtained-
Nanak is ever a sacrifice to the Lord."
(Gauri Sukhmani Mohalla 5, 11-8, p-278)

WHAT TO MEDITATE UPON OR
HOW TO DO PRAISE AND PRAYER:

A sikh is to worship only One God and None else. But God is Formless, what to meditate upon? During the dialogue with the Sidhas, Yogi Charpat asked Guru Nanak, "O Guru, you say that one should not renounce the world rather live in it but the element of Maya (materialism) is so powerful, how can one overcome it and become one with God while living in Maya itself? Please explain your logic behind it."

"The great sea of life is hard to cross, pray tell us how to get safely across it."

(Sidh Gosht- Charpat, p-938)

Guru Nanak gave two examples:

A lotus flower always floats above the surface of the water. It cannot exist without water, yet it remains unaffected by the waves, always rising above the water level. A duck swims in the water but remains and stays above it for fear of drowning.

In the same way a person cannot live without Maya (materialism) in the world, yet while living in it, we are to live above Maya. Material needs are desired and are necessary to sustain the very vital functions of life. Therefore, as a lotus flower and duck do not drown in the water while living in it, a person should remain detached and disinterested with Maya, not forgetting God. That is possible through praise and prayer. Communion with Sabad (Divine Word) will suppress the element of Maya and would enshrine Nam within oneself which in turn would lead a person back into the Unmanifest One:

"As the lotus flower remains unaffected in water
As also a duck swims in it and is not drenched by water
So with fixed intent on Sabad realizing Nam
O Nanak, the dreadful world ocean is crossed safely."
(Ramkali Mohalla 1, Sidh Gosht, 5, p-938)

To achieve an objective in life, a complete attention and dedication is required. The purity of mind and the sincerity of purpose are the requisites to obtain such mission. This task becomes more and more difficult when the object is Formless God. When we recite Gurbani (Sikh Holy Scripture), and if we do not know the meaning of the Sabad (Word or stanza) which is being recited, our meditation becomes mechanical, formalistic and hence futile. The result cannot be positive. Secondly, even if we know the meaning of the Sabad, but our mind is not in the Sabad and it keeps wandering away while we are reciting the Sabad, the outcome will not be significant. **One must, therefore, remember that Prayer**

with absent mindedness will not be fruitful and thereby not acceptable to the Lord. Attentive, alert and completely untainted mind is
required for meditation.

Thus, whenever we read, hear or sing Gurbani (Sabad - a
stanza from Scripture), we must put our whole ATTENTION IN
THE MEANING OF THE SABAD, which is being read, heard or
sung. As our Attention of Mind and Sabad become one, our mind
starts taking the impact of the spirit of the Sabad and the result of
this COMMUNION IS BLISS, PEACE AND EVERLASTING
JOY. In this communion one experiences a taste of Heavenly Elixir
(Hari Ras):

> "O man, all other 'Rasas' (things of relish) thou tasteth
> Satiate not thy thirst even for a moment.
> But if thou ever tasteth the Heavenly Elixir
> Thou shalt be simply wonder-struck."
>
> (Gauri Guareri Mohalla 5, p-180)

When the communion of mind with Sabad is established, **the disciple is reborn in the spirit of the Guru.** He then blends with the Word
(Sabad), and never faces death[2] after this spiritual rebirth:

> "He who dies in the Word, never dies again
> And his devotion becomes fruitful."
>
> (Rag Sorath, Slok Mohalla 3, p-649)

Those who establish communion with Sabad (Gurbani - Divine
Word), shall certainly experience uninterrupted Bliss:

> **"He will become holy, holy, holy, shalt undoubtedly be holy
> O Nanak, who uttereth Nam with heartfelt love."**
>
> (Gauri Sukhmani Mohalla 5, 12-8, p-279)

2- Never faces death means he is never afraid of the death and his cycle of birth and death
will end.

MEDITATION:

Human mind is suffering from untold miseries and calamities in the world. Nam (Name of God) is the cure of all suffering. **Guru Nanak gave a prescription and stood guarantee to the humanity that whosoever one may be irrespective of caste, creed, race, sex, color, religion or nationality:**

> **"He shall become pure whosoever repeateth His(God) Name With devotion, affection and heartfelt love."**

(Gauri Sukhmani Mohalla 5, 20(7), p-290)

The natural tendency of our mind is to wander away hither and thither and not remain absorbed in the Word. So one should bring the mind back into the meaning of the Word while uttering the Sabad (Word).

1.   **Meditate on Gurmantar** - Waahay-Guru **(see below)** means Wonderful God.
      "Waahay-Guru, Waahay-Guru, Waahay-Guru............."

2.   **Then meditate on Mool-mantar:**

Ek-onm-kaar	God is One and Only One
Sat-Naam	(God is) The Eternal Truth
Karta-Purkh	The Almighty Creator
Nirbhao	(He is) Unfearful
Nirvair	(He is) Without hate and enmity
Akaal-Murat	Immortal Entity
Ajuni	Unborn
Saibhang	Self-Existent
Gur-parsaad	(He is) Realized by the Grace of True Guru
	(True Guru is now Divine Word)

**"Ek-onm-kaar Sat-naam Karta-purkh Nirbhao Nirvair
Akaal-murat Ajuni Saibhang Gur-parsaad
Ek-onm-kaar Sat-naam...........................(Repeat)**

(The sound of 'on' in Ek-onm-kaar is not actually like 'on' but it is a
sound like onm
Ek-onm-kaar. It is not actually 'n' but it is mild sound of n like oanm)

SECONDLY: For everyday conduct Guru says:

"Truth is High but higher still is Truthful Living."
(Guru Nanak)
Truthful Living: One must earn one's livelihood by honest means.
No Adultery,
No Tobacco or Drugs,
No Calumny (falseness or misrepresentation).

If it is done with sincerity daily without fail, one will find peace, happiness
and contentment in life.

May God bless us all.

WAHEGURU:

The word, 'WAHEGURU' when appears in Guru Granth Sahib
signifies a devotee's wonder at the Glory of God. This expression is not
an intellectual state of mind but it is at the intuitional level. It is a personal
expression of an individual. He feels and sees lovable, beautiful and at-
tractive attributes of the Eternal around him and his inner self pours out in
adoration. It is a sublime expression of the soul of a devotee to see and
feel His splendors. There are numerous names of God reflecting His attributes and describing His excellences. The extent of God's creation is

also the extent of His names. The name that emerges from a person's own experience and his vision of the Divine is 'WAHEGURU' (pronounced as Waahay-guru) or Wonderful God. It shows a devotee's thrill and enchantment while sensing the magnitude and greatness of His presence. It is a spontaneous, natural and effortless demonstration of an individual's inner feelings. The word 'WAHEGURU' is a Gur-Mantra in Sikhism. It is given by the Guru to the sikhs to meditate upon..

A BRIEF OUTLINE OF FUNDAMENTALS OF SIKHISM

The seed for the reformation of humanity which was sown by Guru Nanak and watered by his successors, ripened in the time of Guru Gobind Singh and culminated in the **creation of the Khalsa.** The sword that carved the Khalsa's way to sublime glory was undoubtedly forged by Guru Gobind Singh but its steel was provided by Guru Nanak. **The whole program of Guru Nanak's initiation reached its exalted state of finality when the tenth Gur Nanak (Guru Gobind Singh) passed on 'Gur Nanak Jot' to the Adi Granth, Holy Scripture- par excellence, and proclaimed it as Guru Granth Sahib, the last Guru for ever (present as well as future).**

From the moment of its initiation by Guru Nanak to the time of its anointment by the tenth Master, Guru Gobind Singh, a period of 239 years, Sikhism acquired its holy scripture, signs and symbols, and form or stance. Guru Nanak was born Guru. He came into this world with heavenly status and with celestial attributes. But all the later Gurus were conferred the Guruship by the previous Gurus. Guru Nanak with his divine power chiseled his own image and installed his Jot in Bhai Lehna who became Guru Angad Dev. The same process of bestowing Guruship went on till Guru Gobind Singh seated the Adi Granth on the spiritual throne of Guru Nanak and declared it as Guru for Ever. Transformation from one Guru to the other happened in the same way as one lamp were to lit from another. The holy transformation of ten Gurus is recognized as ONE, since all of them came from the same Divine Flame in continuation of the same Divine Mission. Guru Nanak established Guruship to perpetuate and preserve the spiritual transmission of its message and to disseminate his teaching in the centuries to come. The concept of Guruship and a hierarchical chain of preceptors was familiar in other religious traditions. But Guru Nanak gave Guruship a new form and content. He gave to the Sikhs an uninterrupted spiritual leadership. In this step he was not followed by any other reformer. He revitalized religion and morality, also was alone in creating a distinct socio-religious community which was destined to play a fruitful and glorious role in India's history. The establishment of Guruship, the story of succession, the founding of Amritsar and other seats of Sikhism, the compilation of the Adi Granth, the institution of Sangat (holy congregation) and Pangat (Guru's free kitchen), the martyrdom of the Gurus, its dignified attire which is a symbol of power, the investiture of the Khalsa, all these and many other events which make the Sikh chronicle, give Sikh religion a color of the highest distinction.

In Sikhism, Guruship does not stand for mere order of mystics, since the Guru attached no value to renunciation of worldly life. Those who practiced renunciation such as Yogis and Sidhas were condemned as shirkers of responsibilities- they were considered as escapists and runaways from social responsibilities and obligations. In Sikhism a man is called upon to accept the Will of God with dedicated submission which requires continuous effort and thus, face suffering and loss with composure and high spirit.

ETHICAL AND MORAL TEACHINGS:

Guru Nanak established three main features for everyday conduct:

1. Naam Japo: Constant rememberance of God (meditation). The whole base and foundation of Sikhism is Naam.
2. Kirat Karo: Earn your livelihood by honest means.
3. Vand Chhako: In His Name share the fruits of your labor as an expression of love and compassion for mankind.

It is further emphasized:

a) Truthful Living: The entire edifice of Sikh Religion is built on turthful living. Guru says, "Truth is high but higher still is truthful living."
(Sri Raag Moh. 1, p-62, Guru Granth Sahib)

b) Moral Restraint: Adultry is absolutely prohibited in Sikh Religion.
c) Do not smoke or indulge in drugs.
d) Do not indulge in Calumny (falseness or misrepresentation).

PILGRIMAGES- Bathing at Holy Places:

A great deal of emphasis on rituals had been the way of Indian religious life for the millions before Guru Nanak appeared on the scene. Wherever Guru Nanak went, he tried to emancipate the masses from the shackles of superstition and ignorance, and instil faith in One All-Pervading and Formless God. At that time people believed that bathing in the river Ganges and other holy places would absolve them of their sins. The Guru asserted that mere bathing at these sacred places, would not cleanse the mind riddled with the impurity of egoism.

'Wandering through the pilgrim places,
One is not rid of one's maladies.
There can be no peace without Nam.'
                (Ramkali Mohalla 1, p-906, Guru Granth Sahib)

The Guru stressed that no abiding peace could be achieved without meditating on Divine Name. Meditation on Nam is the only true pilgrimage:

'Shall we go to bathe at the pilgrim places?
No. Nam is the only true pilgrimage.
Pilgrimage is the contemplation on the Word
That gives inner spiritual light.'
                (Dhanasri Mohalla 1, p-687)

The Guru emphasizes the futility of rushing to the sacred bathing places for the expiation of sins. Guru Nanak states in Japji that he would bathe at the spots considered sacred, if it could please the Lord. The implication is that such ceremonies by themselves would not win God's approbation, without cultivating the moral life.

CASTE SYSTEM AND SOCIAL EQUALITY:

In an age when class distinction was very rigid and when the bonds of caste system in India had strictly divided the people, Guru Nanak taught equality and brotherhood. The Guru rose above rites and rituals, above creeds and conventions, above all national-cults and all race-cults, to a vision of the deeds of love. He preached a religion of love, sacrifice and service. Complete equality among individuals was declared by the Sikh Gurus to be the fundamental moral principle required to regulate the social relations and communication.

The Guru points out that there is no fundamental difference among men of different castes in terms of physical constitution. In a polemical discussion with the Brahmins, Kabir inquires:

"How are you a Brahmin and I am a low caste?
Is it that I have blood in my veins and you have milk?"

(Gauri Kabir p-324)

This exposes the absurdity of any contention or a claim by the higher caste people that there are physical differences among the different castes.

The Guru points out that the laws of nature do no react differently in respect to the higher caste people. Since the nature makes no discrimination in favor of the higher caste by recognizing their superiority in any manner, the myth of caste superiority is clearly seen as man-made. The Guru states:

"What merit is in caste?
The real truth is that he who tastes the poison will die."

(Var Majh, Mohalla 1, p-142)

The Guru vehemently regards caste as an abnormality and social perversity when he says:

"Every one says there are four castes, but it is from God that
every one comes;
The same is the clay which fashions the whole world;
The five elements make up the body's form, and who can say
who has less of these or who has more?"

(Rag Bhairon Mohalla 3, p-1128)

The Guru denies that caste was prevalent from the beginning. In the primitive state:

"No man of caste or birth could be seen ....
There was no distinction of color or coat or of the Brahmin"
                              or Kashatriya......."

(Maru Mohalla 1, p-1035-36)

The claim that the different caste men had emanated from the different parts of the Primeval Man is also repudiated by the Guru:

"His caste is castelessness. He is incarnated not, He is
Self-Existent Existent.......
All hearts are illuminated by the Light of the Lord...."

(Sorath Mohalla 1, 1-2 of 6, p-597)

The Guru, thus, refuses to accredit the caste institution in social ethics and further denies God having favored a few by bringing them out from the higher parts of His body. (These were some of the arguments of the Brahmins to have superiority from birth over low castes).

Finally it is held by the Guru that the caste is of no consideration in the spiritual realization, that human beings of lower caste need not wait to be born again in the next higher class for the attainment of deliverance:

'Whosoever contemplates on God, caste or no caste,
he becomes a blessed devotee of God."

(Basant Mohalla 4, p-1178)

The tenth Master, Guru Gobind Singh, declared caste a taboo in the order of the Khalsa. In Akal Ustat, he states," There is no consideration of caste or membership of varnas." He further writes, "I shall not adopt the habits of any creed, but shall sow the seeds of the pure love of God." (Vachitar Natak, chap. 6, verse 34). The first of the Sikhs baptized into the order of the Khalsa belonged to different castes. The theory of separate duties for different castes was replaced by the same ethical and religious duties for all. Therefore, the fundamental equality of all men was ensured by free and voluntary admission into the order of the Khalsa.

Social Equality:

Wealth also provides a determinant of social classes as against birth in the case of caste system. In Sikhism the relation among classes based on economic resources is envisaged in terms of equality. It rejects the notion of superiority of the economically better placed class over others. The Guru says:

"The man who knoweth God looketh on all men as equal,
As the wind bloweth on the commoner and the king alike."

(Gauri Sukhmani Mohalla 5, 8-1, p-272)

Thus in Sikhism the higher classes are not governed by any separate code of ethics, but all people, rich or poor, are entitled to equal judgment, value and social equality. Since the death is the leveler, the Guru highlights this notion:

"One lives not for ever in the world;
Neither king nor beggar would remain, they all come and go."

(Ramkali Mohalla 1, 11, p-931)

Therefore improper consideration of the superiority of rank are based on a wrong conception. The need for the recognition of human dignity, irrespective of economic classes, is also stressed in an anecdote from the biography of Guru Nanak called the story of Bhai Lalo and Malik Bhago. In that incident Guru Nanak refused a rather sumptuous dinner of Malik Bhago for the ordinary bread of the coarse grain of Bhai Lalo. The moral is drawn that the poor ought not to be treated as low, all must be treated as equal irrespective of their material resources.

STATUS OF WOMEN:

The position of a woman in the society of India, has not been always the same. While at times she had been accorded a very high status, there are also historical and scriptural instances when under some influences, she has been relegated to an inferior position. At the start of Sikhism the status of women was very low in Indian society.

In Sikhism it is considered preposterous to regard woman a 'temptress' or 'seductress' or 'unclean'. The Guru does not regard 'woman' as an obstruction on the way to ultimate goal of Eternal Bliss. This being so, the Guru rejects asceticism or renunciation, and regards the house-holder's life if it is led in a righteous manner, superior to that of a hermit. By emphasizing this type of vision to the people, the Guru stresses that women should be given honorable status in every social and religious segment of the society. Guru Nanak asserted that women were not at all inferior to men:

"From the woman is our birth, in the woman's womb are we shaped;
To the woman we are engaged, to the woman we are wedded;
The woman is our friend and from the woman is the family;
If one woman dies, we seek another, through the woman are the bonds of the world;
Why call woman evil who gives birth to kings?
From the woman comes the woman, without woman there is none;
O Nanak, God alone is the one Who is independent of the woman (because He is unborn)."
(Var Asa Mohalla 1, 2-19, p-473)

This declaration shows unequivocally the high esteem in which a woman's status is held in Sikhism. Woman 'the mother of mighty heroes' is elevated to the highest position in the hierarchy of beings.

In the moral codes of the Sikhs a large number of injunctions deal with the rejection of unethical practices like- (i) female infanticide; (ii) immolation of the widow (Sati) with the deceased husband, and (iii) wearing of veils by women. In the ancient India, it was stated according to spiritual authority that self-immolation on the funeral pyre of her husband was the only honorable course that a virtuous woman could follow; not only would such a woman enjoy eternal bliss in heaven along with her husband, but her action would expiate the sins of three generations of her husband's family both on his father's and mother's side.

Guru Amar Das, the third Master, carried out a vigorous campaign against this practice of Sati, and thereby he emancipated the women from this social oppression and religious cruelty. The Guru declared that "the Sati is one who lives contented and embellishes herself with good conduct, and cherishes the Lord ever and calls on Him." (Rag Suhi, Slok Mohalla 3, 2-6, p-787)

One of the social improvements was the emancipation of women. Many women found salvation through the Guru's teachings. In Sikhism widow remarriage is also permitted whereby the widow can be rehabilitated if she so desires.

INSTITUTIONS OF SANGAT AND PANGAT:

SANGAT- Society of the Holy:

Sangat means assembly or congregation, but in Sikhism Sangat is usually called Sat Sangat (holy congregation) which may be defined as the Home of Truth where people love God and learn to live in Him:

'How should we know of Sat Sangat?
Where the lovers of Truth hold communion with One Lord alone.'
(Sri Rag Mohalla 1, p-72)

Again the fourth Guru gives definition of Sangat:

"Sat Sangat is the school of the True Guru,
There we learn to love God and appreciate His greatness."
(Var Kanra Mohalla 4, p-1313)

Guru Nanak attached great importance to the setting up of Sangats, the holy assemblies, and wherever he went, he tried to establish them. The Divine Word (Gurbani) and the Sat Sangat were the only two means that the Guru employed to rid the people of their selfishness and evil passions; and finally for their salvation and for uniting them with God:

"Sat Sangat is the treasury of Divine Name;
There we meet God;
Through the Grace of Guru,
One receives there Light and all darkness is dispelled."

(Sarang ki Var, Mohalla 4, p-1244)

Wherever Guru Nanak went, the Sikhs built Gurdwara (house of the Guru). They met there every day and formed into a regular Sangat. From the time of the third Master, Guru Amar Das, it was felt that the Sikhs should have their own seats of religion. He founded the town of Chak Ram Das which subsequently got its present name, Amritsar; and he got a Bawli (a well with staircase reaching down to the water surface) constructed at Goindwal. The fourth and fifth Masters also showed great interest in building up new religious centers for their followers such as Amritsar, Kartarpur etc. These religious centers formed a great cementing force for the rising Sikh community. The Sikh Sangats from far and near used to visit these centers and had the opportunity of not only meeting the Holy Guru and having his blessings, but also coming into close contact with one another. During their visit they were provided with free accommodation and free food. Simron (participation in daily religious service) and seva (participation in the community projects and Guru ka Langar, kitchen) were the two major parts of the daily routine of the visiting Sikhs. These close contacts formed the bases of a well-integrated Sikh organization.

The process of integration of Sikhism went hand in hand with the enlargement of its ranks. During the time of the third Guru, there were twenty-two manjis and fifty-two piris, which were all big and small centers for the spread of Sikh religion in the country. Guru Ram Das, the fourth Master, established a new order of missionaries called Masands. This new order was reorganized and elaborated by the fifth Guru. As the number of new Sikh Sangats grew larger in the country, the mode of initiation of prospective Sikhs through the ceremony of Charanpauhal (Charanamrit - see Appendix under Glossary) was allowed to all authorized missionaries. Although the ideal Charanamrit was the one administered by the Guru himself, since it was not possible for the Guru to be present physically everywhere, the authority of initiation was delegated to local missionaries. The bulk of the people who came to the fold of Sikhism as a result of the above efforts, were drawn from the commercial classes mostly dwelling in the towns. During the period of the fifth Guru, the movement became popular in the country side also, with the result that a large number of Majha Jats embraced Sikhism.

Finances are very necessary for the success of any movement. In the beginning, the voluntary offerings of the devotees were sufficient. When big projects were undertaken, the existing practice was found inadequate. In order to meet the situation, the masands were required not merely to concentrate on the dissemination of Sikh teachings, but also to collect donations from the faithful and to bring them to the headquarters of the Guru.

PANGAT- Guru's Free Kitchen known as Langar:

Another institution of Pangat or Langar (free common kitchen) was organized almost simultaneously with that of Sangat. It was initiated by Guru Nanak and its consolidation and extension was affected by the third Guru. The rules of the Langar require that all should sit in the same row and partake of the same food without any distinction of high or low, rich or poor, and prince or the peasant. It was the injunction of Guru Amar Das that none could have his audience unless he had eaten in the Langar. When the Raja of Haripur or even Emperor Akbar, came to see the Guru, they had to sit with other common people and dine together with them before the Master gave consent to see them. In this way the people were made to renounce their social prejudices. Common kitchen also served as a medium of social integration.

The institution of Pangat imparted a secular dimension to the Sangat. **Most importantly it translated the principle of equality into practice, and it also served as a uniting force among the followers of Sikhism.** This institution provides safeguard against the immoral social practice of untouchability which is a by-product of the caste system. **It is a sin against God Who made the same blood flow in all human veins and a crime against humanity.**

This institution is run with the help and contributions of all and not by any one particular person or class of persons. The free kitchen where prince and peasant could mess together, fostered a spirit of charity on a large scale and also became a powerful binding force.

CONCEPT OF KARMA IN SIKHISM:

Theory of Karma: Karma means action. Every action is associated with its result. Actions of human beings are of paramount importance in determining their destiny. Therefore, deeds good or bad write the script of a person's future. The effects of a person's behavior are operative not only in this life but in life after death also. He is slave to his past. Our present existence has resulted from what we did in our previous lives and what we do now, will regulate our next life. From doctrine of Karma originates the theory of rebirth of the soul. Karma of a person is based on the assumption of continuity of the soul after death. It is a continuous cycle of rebirth and death. The ephemerality of a single span of life is too inconsistent to give any person a chance to attain perfection and spiritual excellence. Closed road for the soul and limiting it to one life would mean religious ventures and endeavors of humanity are all meaningless and absurd.

According to the dictum, "As you sow, so shall you reap," Karma alone is ultimate and its retribution never fails. God cannot interfere in the working of its mechanism. Existence or non-existence of God has no significance. This is associated with the atheistic school of thought. Such a belief reduces the functioning of an individual to a mere mechanical model. Human being with all the mental faculties cannot pull himself up by his own bootstraps and is not free to work towards salvation of his own soul. Wicked deeds of his previous life stand in the way of his freedom. This concept of retribution strikes a chord of dark pessimism in human heart because the soul finds no opportunity to get out of its present predicament.

Sikhism believes in the concept of continuity of the soul after death in different forms, human or animal. It accepts the theory of law of Karma along with the idea of retribution. But it is not taken to be absolute or inexorable. The rigidity of Karma is repulsive to Sikh thought as it does not recognize the merciful trait of the Almighty God. He being the Absolute Arbiter may write off the effects of all malicious actions of a person thereby asserting His supremacy over Karma. According to Sikh faith though Karma is important force in life, its web is not so intricate as to exclude the possibility of redemption of human soul. **To obtain celestial peace and to offset the weight of offensive and loathsome deeds Sikhism demands strict observance of all its prescriptions. It offers happy immortality and life without despair and melancholy to its faithful. Singing the Glory of God erases the blot of thousands of evil deeds of the past and present life. Repeating God's Name can redeem a repentant sinner. Bhagat Ravidas in one of his devotional hymns so eloquently expressed his thought which is incorporated in Sikh Holy Scripture (Guru Granth Sahib):**
     "Were we not sinners, how would Thou then be called the redeemer of the fallen!"
God's Word is like a lamp which when lighted inside the human heart, gives the light by consuming the oil of suffering. Such is the Splendor of God's Grace and Compassion. Therefore, according to Sikh Scripture the law of Karma ceases to operate. In Sikh monotheistic concept, Absolute and Supreme Power is held in highest reverence.

Theory of Transmigration: It is the rebirth of human soul in descending order. Because of moral failings of an individual in previous life, the soul passes through various animal lives suffering untold miseries. It is a punishment and a curse for a person's wicked deeds in previous human birth. In Sikh scripture these sinister actions are compared to chains around the neck, fetters on the legs and to hangman's noose. **The soul carries the load of its sins from one lower life to another and groans under its own burden. It is an intense agonizing ordeal. No researcher, explorer nor any scientist with their accumulated knowledge can bring an emancipation of the soul from this continuous cycle of suffering.** If the law of Karma was absolutely inexorable, human soul would have been eternally doomed and would have no chance of extricating itself out of the cycle of transmigration. **Sikhism offers annulment from transmigration of the soul through repeating God's Name in all awareness in this life and by leading a sublime and truthful life.** Guru Nanak says, "Truth is high but higher still is truthful living." Practice of praising the Glory of the Lord is the highest of all practices and in return it purges out all sins of human beings.

Reincarnation: According to Sikh creed a soul before getting this human body, has passed through several lives of lower species. Therefore, this life is precious and a gift of God. It means God out of compassion and mercy has given the soul one more chance to improve itself spiritually and terminate the bondage of transmigration. It is an opportunity to attain union with God which is the mission of Sikhism. If a soul fails to obtain liberation in this life then in accordance with its good deeds, it will be reborn in human form. Reincarnation is rebirth of human soul in ascending order. It passes from one human life to another in its spiritual and moral progress. Soul is reborn in human form for its further development. In each rebirth it gets better opportunities to improve on its virtues. Good deeds will ensure a person rebirth in a station of life where the achievement of liberation of the soul will be facilitated. It goes on acquiring human births till it eliminates rebirth completely and attains eternal peace by merging with the Supreme Soul. To get reincarnated is to lead this life without sin and with full devotion to God. According to a school of thought the doctrine of reincarnation is considered to be too individualistic because a person is determined on achieving emancipation of his own soul no matter what happens to his family and community in the process. Individual works towards his own spiritual perfection only.

Sikh divine ordinance does not establish a person's destiny but only lays down moral laws and human being's actions are measured accordingly. **There is divine justice.**
Daily conduct and performances decide how a person stands in the ultimate count with the Creator. God is responsible for the existence of evil by the side of good. These are part of His creation and are governed by the laws created by Him. But He is not responsible for moral anarchy in an individual's life. Poverty of moral values leads to impurities in mental state resulting in spiritual degeneration. This will generate evil and moral crisis in an individual's life. People suffer for their evil actions because evil is negation of God's Will and are rewarded for their good behavior in the court of His Kingdom. Human being is an ideal representation and crown of His inventions and is the only creature of this cosmic existence who is capable of conscious volition and can organize his daily activities to attain good over evil. **Therefore, a person is accountable for any lapses from morality.** Because of his mental capabilities he is considered to be sovereign and sufficient in his powers and is expected to advance to the loftiest peaks of spiritual glory which is the goal established by Sikh Divinity for its followers.

FEAR IN SIKHISM:

Sikhs are exhorted by their Gurus to cultivate noble and virtuous qualities in their hearts which are identified with the spiritual ideals.. One of them is 'fear', cherishing fear of none but of God only, the Creator and the Sustainer of life. Fear of God in human heart is different from worldly horror or panic. Fear of the Almighty does not mean just 'awe'. It is not an instinctive shrinking back from earthly danger. **But it is the tremor of the soul lest one should do by word, deed or thought anything that may be against the Will of God.** Any wicked deed or thought is the negation of the Will of the Supreme Lord. It is opposing His Glory and

Splendor. Evil is a hurdle for the human soul during its journey leading to His kingdom. Therefore, it should be wiped out completely from human heart. Fear of God should be out of love and honor for Him. Holding Him in such a high esteem that going against His Will shakes the core of a person's heart. Tribute should be paid to Him out of love and dread of His Mighty power. Such is the fear that Sikh religion inculcates in its followers. It is a great quality that lifts a devotee to a status of morally and spiritually oriented personality. This leads an individual towards spiritual excellence and finally attaining it. Elegance of a devotee lies in the fact that he is always inspired by such a fear of God. It is this fear of Him and dread of His Name that burns off all our sins as fire burns the straw. With such a fear of the Lord we can cross the worldly ocean of pain and suffering. Prompted by this an individual can achieve higher and Godly attributes which is the goal of Sikh Faith.

> "Without the Lord's fear, one can worship Him not, nor love the
>   Lord's Name.
> Meeting with the True Guru, Lord's fear wells up and one is
>   embellished with
>   the Love-in-fear of God."
>   (Var Suhi Mohalla 3, pauri(9), p-788)

UNIVERSAL BROTHERHOOD:

The ideal of social equality is not the ultimate aim of the ethics of Sikhism. This equality may be maintained without feeling any affection or regard for each other, but such bare equality would not be enough because it does not conform to the ideal of humanistic morality. Hence in order to make it whole, it should be saturated with the idea of spiritual unity of mankind. The Guru stated:

"As out of a single fire, millions of sparks arise; arise in

separation but come together again when they fall back in the fire. As from a heap of dust, grains of dust sweep up and fill the air, and filling it fall in a heap of dust. As out of single stream,
countless waves rise up and being water, fall back in water again. So from God's form emerge alive and inanimate things and since they arise from Him, they shall fall in Him again."

(Guru Gobind Singh-Akal Ustat)

This means that every human being deserves to be treated as a member of the same human brotherhood. The fellow human being is not an 'other'. The Guru says:

"Meeting with the Guru, I have abandoned the sense of the otherness."

(Bhiro Mohalla 5, 1-29-42, p-1148)

The other is in fact not an 'other' but a co-sharer of the same source and a part of the same spiritual order. This sense of brotherhood of humanity is, thus, linked together by bonds deeper than family, social or national affinities. This brotherhood of mankind in terms of God being the common father is stressed by the Guru:

"Thou art the father of us all........all are the partners, Thou art alien to none."

(Majh Mohalla 5, p-97)

The Guru is pointing to the common bonds of existence in the world:

"Air is the Guru, water is father, great earth the mother; In the lap of two nurses, night and day, the whole world is brought up."

(Japji, Slok, p-8)

According to the Guru, the brotherhood is the reality but it is hidden from us by the veil of houmai (I-am-ness or individuation). Houmai is the dirt over our mind which it has gathered during the process of transmigration. Once this dirt over our mind is removed and the veil of houmai (I-am-ness) is broken, the relationship across the human lines becomes a clear reality. As long as our minds remain under the veil of I-am-ness, our understanding will continue to be hollow and away from reality. How do we clean our mind?

As mentioned before the Guru gives direction how to clean the mind:
"Only through praise and prayer to God
Mind will become pure."

(Wadhans Mohalla 1, p-557)

Once mind becomes pure, it attains a spiritual height in which reality opens up and all delusion is gone and then sense of universal brotherhood prevails:
"There is One father of us all
And we are children of the same father."

(Sorath Mohalla 5, p-611)

"I am neither a Hindu nor a Muslim;
The soul and body belong to God whether He be called Allhah or Ram."

(Bhairo Mohalla 5, p-1136)

This is the desired mental stage commanded by the Guru when a person's mind is lifted above the lines of religion, color, race or national entity; and the sense of real universal brotherhood is born:
"There is no enemy, none is 'other',
A sense of universal brotherhood has come to me."

(Kanra Mohalla 5, p-1299)

Sikhism believes in it, stands for it and takes practical measures to realize it. There are numerous examples in the Sikh history to emphasize this fact.

Guru Nanak traveled for fourteen years on foot and he covered the area from Assam Hills in the east of India to as far as Iran and Iraq in the west; from Tibet in the north to Ceylon in the south. During this long journey he went to various famous Hindu temples and their learning centers, Maths of Sidhas, and the various centers of Mohammadans including Mecca, and delivered the Divine Message (brotherhood of mankind and Fatherhood of God) for which he came to this world. Never he asked any one to become his disciple in order to go to heaven. He rather held guarantee to the entire humanity that if a person, irrespective of race, color, caste, creed, sex, religion or nationality, meditates on God, the Formless One, will get deliverance:

'He shall become pure, whosoever repeateth His Name
With devotion, affection and heartfelt love."

(Gauri Sukhmani Mohalla 5, 20-7, p-290)

Sikhism fully stands for universal brotherhood in word and in spirit. Every Sikh living in every corner of the world when he prays in the morning and in the evening, ends his prayer by saying:

"By Thy Grace, may every one be blessed in the world."

MORAL LIFE:

According to Sikh faith moral life is not just a combination of rituals, ceremonial acts nor certain codes. Neither it is a blend of ethical norms. But it is a life lived with divine approval filled with heroism to live and die for pious ideals frustrating evil. Here heroism is implied as waging battle against the lower impulses. Moral life is the fruit of spiritual purity which is a spiritual ascent and journey of human soul towards achieving union with the Divine. It is the result of religious illumination where all the finer emotions and sublime ideas are cultivated. It is an accomplishment reached through religious discipline which curbs the actions that lead to sin. Meditation on the Absolute One illuminates the mind which in return annuls the poisons of evil resulting in moral life. By living under the influence of religion mind's restlessness ceases and moral life emerges. It is the outcome of truthful conduct which is a sovereign virtue. It is not an exercise at the intellectual level but is a fulfillment of the intuition. It is a life lived with staunch belief that **He is without any equal and deep faith that from His terror the wind blows, the rivers flow and the sun and the moon move in their orbits.**

Sikhism is not a dogma but a way of life lived according to Guru Rahit Maryada (code of conduct). A Sikh has to

hold his Guru's word as paramount in his daily existence. Without glorifying His presence in one's existence, life will be contaminated and polluted and will be in deplorable state which will lead to spiritual degeneration. Deep and continuous contemplation on Nam is needed and is indispensable for the exalted state of Sikh character. Nam is neither a philosophy nor knowledge to be gained from books. It dwells within and is realized from within through the grace of the true Guru (Gurbani - Divine Word). Let the following be our daily supplication:

"O my friend, the Divine Guru!
Illuminate my mind with the Name Divine!
Let the Name revealed to me by the Guru be my life-companion;
And singing Thy Glory be my daily routine."
(Rag Gujri Mohalla 4, p-10, Guru Granth Sahib)

EXCELLENCES OF RELIGION:

Religion is faith and not science. It is not found in books neither in theory nor in learned arguments nor in logical reasoning nor in ascetic way. But it is a life full of virtues and merits with devotion to God amidst all the worldly desires and temptations. It is both a commitment and the way in which that commitment is fulfilled in human life. When religion forms an indispensable part of one's life, it ensures a calm, adorable and angelic development of personality. The need for a teacher does not end with academic career. It is a life long requirement. Religion is a teacher and a guide for a person steering him away from undesirable worldly pitfalls. It is an aid to richer and fuller life generating a climate of spiritual and moral values in an individual's existence resulting in the attainment of godly attributes. Every faith teaches to glorify God through hymns and narratives. This helps to reflect and meditate on His Excellences. By doing so such an attitude of mind is developed by which one would constantly be living in

Divine presence. Religion reinforces and satisfies thirst and hunger of human soul for the Divine. It should not be allowed to fall into a sad neglect because this will result in erosion of human values. Poverty and decay of these values will create moral crises in individuals leading to spiritual bankruptcy and moral anarchy in society. Cultivating religious beliefs and values can root out from a person's mind the human capacity for evil. It helps in purification of human heart from sinfulness.

Since the start of human race, humanity is conscious of religion. No society, tribe nor clan is known to exist without religion. It has been depicted by people through art, architect, hymns and songs. Any pious and devout community or society which does not guard its religious values indicates a lower level of development. A society is considered to be progressive when it reflects its spiritual and religious legacy. That system of beliefs and religious values which were held with ardor and faith by our ancestors is deemed to disappear in the long run if not preserved in its original and traditional order. Discarding of these precious values without replacement by other system equally valuable is bound to result in social crisis. No society can aspire to build up a superstructure of moral progress without a stable, social and religious order. The new industrial society and forces of modernism and science should not be permitted to imperil basic values which ought to govern the society. Our world is going through some very difficult and dangerous times. With no violence but armed with religion- God's Word, we all can cross through painful suffering and distresses of present days. A majority of eastern religions have put so much currency in it that in some of their highly celebrated and documented verses, they have evaluated human life without any ray of religion as contaminated, polluted and accumulative waste. As crop is ruined without rain, similarly without religion our souls will wither away.

BIBLIOGRAPHY

PUNJABI

1. Guru Granth Sahib
2. Bhai Gurdas- Varan
3. Bhai Vir Singh- Santhia Sri Guru Granth Sahib
4. Dr. Kartar Singh- Sikh Fundamentals
5. Prof. Sahib Singh- Jiwan Birtant of the Gurus
6. Guru Granth Sahib by Bhai Manmohan Singh

ENGLISH

7. Avtar Singh- Ethics of the Sikhs
8. Gandhi, Surjeet Sigh- History of the Sikh Gurus
9. Guru Granth Sahib- English Translation by
   Bhai Manmohan Singh
10. Guru Granth Sahib- English Translation by Dr. Gopal Singh
11. Guru Granth Sahib- English Translation by Principal
    G. S. Talib
12. Harbans Singh- Perspectives on Guru Nanak
13. Kohli S.S.- Outline of Sikh Thought
14. Macauliffe, M.A.- The Sikh Religion Vol. 1-6
15. Ranbir Singh- Glimpses of the Divine Masters
16. Ranbir Singh- The Sikh Way of Life
17. Sikhism- Fauja Singh, Trilochan Singh,
    Gurbachan Singh Talib, J.P. Singh Oberoi, Sohan Singh
18. SIKH RELIGION by Sikh Missionary Center

APPENDIX

TURBAN:

Turban is an integral part of an attire of a Sikh. Whenever you come across a person with beard and turban, most probably he is a Sikh from India. Many Muslims as well as many Hindus wear turbans in India but every Sikh who has beard and long hair, must wear turban. It is by the order of the Guru that a Sikh is required not to cut hair and keep the natural appearance intact. When we have beard and long hair, it has become religiously mandatory in Sikhism to wear turban. A Sikh cannot go to any place without wearing turban. Turban is an important part of dress and mandatory headgear. Like others it is not a symbol or icon but it is essential part of dress of a Sikh. In today's civilized world every religion has a place and Sikhism is the fifth largest religion in the world. Sikhs are the most visible minority and their turban is the most distinctive identifying mark of their religious belief and practice.

GURDWARA: A Sikh church is called Gurdwara (House of the Guru). Anybody irrespective of caste, creed, race, color, sex, religion or nationality, can enter the Gurdwara and join the services. Doors of the Gurdwara are open equally to all human beings. There are four doors to the complex of the Golden Temple (the highest seat of Sikh Religion at Amritsar in India) which signifies that all the four castes have equal access to the Guru's House (the Golden Temple) and also that God pervades neither only in the east nor only in the west but equally in all the four directions. One does not have to become a member or pay dues to be part of the services in the Gurdwara. Before entering the Gurdwara hall, one has to cover head and take shoes off as a traditional respect to the Guru. Guru Granth Sahib is installed at a higher platform. All who enter, bow before it and make offerings. These offerings are made to the Holy Guru and are

Guru Granth Sahib in State

Raagis doing Kirtan

Holy Congregation- men sitting on one side

Women sitting on the opposite side
in the hall of the Gurdwara

utilized for the religious objectives. Whenever Guru Granth Sahib is kept in state, an attendant (**Granthi or priest**) waves the fly-whisk (**Chauri**) over it. Over it, is spread a canopy or awning to mark its sacred character. All sit on the floor in a praying attitude, men on one side while women occupy exactly the opposite side as being equal. The Holy Congregation is called **Sadh Sangat.** As mentioned before, Guru Granth Sahib is in poetic form, the musicians called **Raagis** sing the hymns from Guru Granth Sahib and that is called **Kirtan.** Thanksgiving for a joyous event or prayers for the peace of the departed soul or in general to express devotion, must be offered in the presence of Guru Granth Sahib. No sikh marriage can be sanctified except in its presence, with bride and groom circumambulating it reverently four times, while the nuptial hymns from its pages are being chanted (**Lavan**). Its affirmations may be invoked for blessings. The principal Sikh religious ceremony consists in making a complete recitation of Guru Granth Sahib (1430 pages) over a number of days, usually a week or ten days, concluding with the holding of congregational prayers, chanting of sacred hymns musically (Kirtan) and distribution of grace-offerings (**Karah Parsad -** pudding made from butter, sugar and wheat flour). This ceremony is called **Bhog**.

Since recent times a non-stop recitation of the Holy Scripture (**Akhand Paath**) followed by Bhog is largely in vogue. The Akhand Paath takes about 48 hours and is usually done by trained priests. Every religious ceremony is concluded by a formal prayer (**Ardaas**) when everybody stands with folded hands and the prayer is said by the head priest. After that a randomly selected passage is read from Guru Granth Sahib which is considered the Divine Order (**Hukam**) of the day and after that Karah Parsad is distributed followed by **Langar** (free meals).

FIVE TAKHATS: Takhat means throne- throne of Sikh Religious Authority-Spiritual as well as Temporal. There are Five Takhats in Sikh Religion:

1. Akal Takhat Sahib, Amritsar (Punjab State, India).
2. Takhat Patna Sahib, Patna (Bihar). Birth place of Tenth Guru.

3. Takhat Kesgarh Sahib, Anandpur (Punjab). Khalsa was created here in 1699.
4. Takhat Hazur Sahib, Nanded (Maharashtra). Tenth Guru breathed his last here.
5. Takhat Damdama Sahib, Talwandi Sabo (Punjab). Tenth Guru dictated Final version of Guru Granth Sahib here.

The head of a Takhat is called **Jathedar.** The Jathedar of Akal Takhat Sahib is the Head Jathedar. Any decision- religious, social or even political, taken by the Five Jathedars in the presence of Guru Granth Sahib, is binding on all the Sikhs. The Five Jathedars under the leadership of the Akal Takhat Sahib Jathedar have the Supreme authority in Sikh Religion.

GURPURB: Important Sikh Celebration Days (Festivals) are:
1. Birthday of First Guru (Guru Nanak Dev) is in November.
2. Birthday of Tenth Guru (Guru Gobind Singh) is in January.
3. Creation of Khalsa (The Order of Baptized Sikhs) is on April 13.
4. Martyrdom day of Fifth Guru (Guru Arjan Dev) is in June.
5. Guruship to Holy Scripture (Guru Granth Sahib) is in October.

SIKH NAMES: When a child is born in Sikh family, a randomly selected passage is read from Guru Granth Sahib (Divine Order). The first letter of the first word of the passage is taken to form a name. For example if the letter is 'G', the name can be Gurdev, Gurcharan, Gurbachan.........
All Sikh men are named as **'SINGH'** (Lion) after the first name like Gurdev Singh...
All Sikh women are named as **'KAUR'** (princess) after the first name like Gurcharan Kaur ......These names (Singh, Kaur) are given by the Guru.

SIKH GREETINGS: A male Sikh is seen wearing turban and beard. When a Sikh meets another Sikh, he (they) greets with folded hands and says:
Wahayguru ji ka Khalsa

Wahayguru ji ki Fateh
(Khalsa belongs to the Glorious Master (God) and All Triumph be to His
Name). Sikhs also usually greet saying, "Sat Siri Akaal" (Truth is Immor-
tal).

SIKH CALENDAR: Sikhs follow the usual Indian Calendar months.
The second month called 'Vaisaakh' begins on April 13. The twelve months
are: Cheit, Vaisaakh, Jeith, Haar (Asar), Sawan, Bhadon, Asu, Katik,
Maghar, Poh (Pokh), Magh and Phalgun.

GLOSSARY OF SIKH WORDS:

Akhand Paath: A non-stop recitation of the Holy Scripture (Guru Granth
Sahib) which takes about 48 hours and is done by trained priests (1430
pages).
Amrit: Sikh Baptism ceremony. Also name given to Nectar prepared in
baptism ceremony.
Anand Karaj: Sikh Marriage ceremony.
Ardaas: A formal prayer after concluding every religious ceremony when
everybody stands with folded hands and the prayer is said by the head
priest.
Bhai: A respectable form of address, literally, 'brother'.
Bhog: (i) Completion of reading of whole of Guru Granth Sahib (1430
          pages) and
          (ii) completion of every day religious ceremony.
Chanani: A canopy is spread over the Holy Scripture whenever the Holy
Guru Granth Sahib is kept in state as a mark of royalty.
Charanpauhal(Charnamrit): This was a form of initiation before the
creation of the Khalsa by drinking the water in which Guru's feet were
washed or Guru's toe was dipped. The preamble of Japji (Moolmantar)
was also read at the same time. This ceremony was inaugurated by the
Guru. Sabad was also given by the Guru to be meditated upon.

Chaur: Whenever Guru Granth Sahib is kept in state, an attendant waves the fly-whisk over it as mark of royalty.

5 K's: Every baptized Sikh must wear the five articles whose names begin with 'k':

1. Kes: not to cut hair. This represents the natural appearance of saintlihood. This is the First token of Sikh Faith.
2. Kanga: A comb to clean the hair.
3. Kachha: A warrior's shorts.
4. Kara: A steel bracelet on the wrist, a symbol of dedication to the Guru..
5. Kirpan: A sword for self-defense and a symbol of dignity, power and unconquerable spirit.

Granthi: The priest who looks after the Gurdwara and Guru Granth Sahib.

Gurmantar: Mantar given by the Guru to his followers to be meditated upon. It is 'Waheguru' in Sikh Religion.

Gurmukhi: Script popularized by second Sikh Guru (Guru Angad Dev) to write Punjabi language and also Guru Granth Sahib.

Hukam: Guru Granth Sahib is opened randomly and first stanza is read from the top of the left page and that is called 'Hukam', the Divine Order of the day.

Karah Prasad: Grace-offering- a pudding made from butter, wheat flour and sugar.

Katha: Religious exposition of Gurbani (Guru Granth Sahib).

Khalsa: The order of baptized Sikhs founded by Guru Gobind Singh in 1699.

Khanda: Literally a double-edged sword. Also the name of a distinctive design that incorporates a double-edged sword used in the emblem of the Khalsa:.

(a) Two-edged sword in the center of the ring. It symbolizes disintegration of false pride and inequalities.

(b) Chakar (an iron ring). It exhorts the Sikhs to serve the whole creation.

(c) Two swords on either side of the Chakar (ring). The two swords represent meeri and peeri (Temporal and Spiritual authority).

Kirtan: Singing of hymns of Guru Granth Sahib.

Langar: Practice of serving free food after the religious ceremony. It was started by the first Guru and strengthened further by the later Gurus. The rules of Langar require that all irrespective of caste, sex, religion or nationality, should sit in the same row and partake of the same food without any discrimination. It really translates the principle of equality into practice.

Lavaan: Circumambulating of the Holy Guru Granth Sahib during the Sikh marriage ceremony.

Moolmantar: It is the opening stanza in Guru Granth Sahib which depicts the Attributes of God - "Ek-onm-kaar Sat-Naam Karta-purkh Nirbhao Nirvair Akaal-murat Ajuni Saibhang Gurparsaad."

Nishan Sahib: Nishan Sahib is the name given to the flag of the Khalsa. It is saffron in color, triangular in shape and the Khanda in black. The flag post is generally covered with saffron cloth and has a metallic khanda at the top. The Nishan Sahib is installed in every Gurdwara (Sikh Church).

Paath: Reading of the Holy Guru Granth Sahib

Panj Payaray: Five Beloved Ones (Five baptized Sikhs).

Panth: The Sikh community as a whole.

Raagis: Musicians who sing hymns of Guru Granth Sahib.

Rumala: A cover cloth placed over the Holy Guru Granth Sahib in between readings.

Sabad (Shabad): Divine Word. A stanza from Guru Granth Sahib.

Sadh Sangat: The Holy congregation.

Sant: Saint.

Seva: Devoted service to humanity.

Sikh: Literally means disciple. Usually a follower of Sikh Religion.